J. W. Meath

Pedestin

A Drama in four Acts

J. W. Meath

Pedestin
A Drama in four Acts

ISBN/EAN: 9783337336882

Printed in Europe, USA, Canada, Australia, Japan

Cover: Foto ©Thomas Meinert / pixelio.de

More available books at **www.hansebooks.com**

PEDESTIN:

A Drama,

IN FOUR ACTS.

BY J. W. ▮▮ATH.

WITH CAST OF CHARACTER▮ ▮▮▮▮▮▮SS, COSTUMES,
RELATIVE PO▮▮▮▮▮▮▮▮TC.

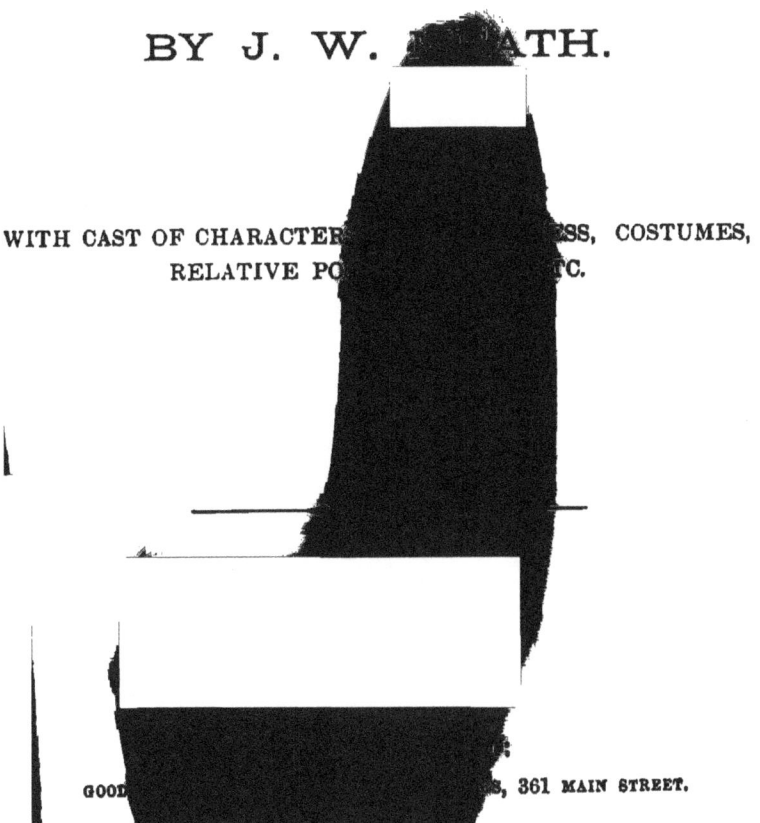

GOOD▮▮▮▮▮▮▮▮▮▮▮▮▮▮▮▮S, 361 MAIN STREET.

LAST OF CHARACTERS.

Cute (the reliable.)
Colonel Nortville.
Joel Mertloff.
Paris Desmer.
Walter Benson (alias Walter Bruce.)
Lawyer Mason.
Landlord of the Half-Way Inn.
Sam Green (a sharper.)
Officer.
Russell.

PEDESTIN.
Rose Merview.
Mrs. Desmer.
Grany Swabs.

COSTUMES.

Of the present day.

SYNOPSIS OF SCENERY.

ACT I.

Scene   I.—*A Cotton-field.*
Scene II.—*Plain Wood.*
Scene III.—*A furnished apartment.*
Scene IV.—*Plain Room.*
Scene   V.—*A Garden.*

ACT II.

Scene   I.—*Same as Scene III Act I.*
Scene II.—*A set Cottage.*
Scene III.—*Plain Chamber.*
Scene IV.—*A Street.*
Scene   V.—*The Cabin of the Steamboat Reindeer.*
Scene VI.—*The Rapids—Steamboat on fire—Storm.*

ACT III.

Scene   I.—*A set Inn (Sign Half-way.)*
Scene II.—*Interior of a Log House denoting strength.*
Scene III.—*Same as Scene I. Act III.*
Scene IV.—*A Precipice–high rocks on both sides, a foot path across. Cataract in the distance.*

ACT IV.

Scene   I.—*Plain Room.*
Scene II.—*A Set Cottage.*
Scene III.—*A Street in the Village.*
Scene IV.—*A furnished apartment.*

Pedestin.

ACT I.

SCENE 1.—*A Cotton Field in open boll. The negroes at work picking it in bags. Large baskets also full of cotton at the end of each row. They sing as they work. The back scene must also in addition to the stage show a cotton-field in view, in order to have the desired effect. (The cotton field must be well up stage so as to allow a walk around and dance of negroes in front.) Cute heard singing in the distance; all join in the chorus.*

Enters CUTE *still singing,* R.

Cute. Look haur, nigs, I'se got de best news to tell you dat you ebber did hear. Yous got dis day fur a holiday, so quit your workin. Missie Patavine has come home from de boardin-school, and Massa Kurnel is gwine to gib all you nigs dis day for frolickin' 'count ob it. I'se so happy dat I—[*He dances.*]

All the niggers. You's only gummin', Uncle Cute. [*They leave work and come down stage.*]

Cute. No, I isen't; for Missie Patavine is at home and looks so sweet and nice—de lobliest gal dat I'se eber seen wid dese two eyes—I'se so glad too, kase Massa Kurnel says I shan't do nuffin but wait on Missie Patavine; so let's honor her comin' by habin' a good old dance. [*A general dance and walk-around by all characters. Exit all singing, except Cute.*] I'se seen Massa Paris in de woods yonder hunting, and I'se agwine and tell him dat Missie Patavine 'rived home dis mornin. Won't he be glad to hear it, dough, kase I knows dat he lubs her. [*Exit* R, *singing.*]

Scene II.—*Plain Woods.*

Enter Paris Desmer, *with gun, game-bag, etc., and* Cute.

Paris. What does all this rejoicing mean, Cute? Something uncommon must call forth this clamor. Is there going to be a double marriage at the quarters, to-night?

Cute. Someting better dan dat, Massa Paris.

Paris. It must be something very important, then!

Cute. Oh! yes, for ebery nig on de plantation is gwine to get dis as a holiday.

Paris. [*Much interested.*] What is it, Cute? Why not tell me?

Cute. Can't you guess, Massa Paris?

Paris. No—how can I guess it?

Cute. Golly, I knows dat you guesses it—does your heart goes pit-a-pat, Massa Paris?

Paris. No—what would make it go pit-a-pat?

Cute. Well, I'll tell you—but is you ready?

Paris. Yes, I'm ready—why don't you out with it?

Cute. Well—would you beliebe dat Missie Patavine 'rived home from school dis morning.

Paris. [*Starts.*] Pedestin at home!

Cute. Yes, and she look so sweet, too, Massa Paris, dat I hardly knows her —jus like a picture—not de wile gal dat she use to be.

Paris. No, I dare say not. [*Aside.*] Time has marked its course in more ways than one, I fear. Yet, why should I countenance a doubt, when I know naught to the contrary.

Cute. Ain't you glad to hear ob her return, Massa Paris, kase I knows you lub de gal.

Paris. As a friend, Cute.

Cute. More dan dat. Don't you 'member how you used to write letters to each odder, and dat I used to be de mail bag to tote dem for you.

Paris. We were both young then, Cute.

Cute. Ole folks has de same feelins, Massa Paris, kase I'se been dar mysef.

Paris. So you have had experience in love matters, have you, Cute?

Cute. I has dat—I'se been a possum among de gals, in my days.

Paris. Did she say anything as to—

Cute. No, Massa Paris, she didn't—de kurnel was dar all de time, and also dat—

Paris. That who?

Cute. Joel Mertloff.

Paris. 'Joel Mertloff, did you say?

Cute. Yes, you knows, Massa Paris, dat I don't like him—'twas him dat told Massa Kurnel about me totin' letters for you and Missie Patavine, and got me whipped.

Paris. Yes, Cute, I do remember that—and it remains yet to be adjusted with him—I hope the day is not far distant when I will—

Cute. And so does I, Massa Paris, for he am eberyting but a gemman, and I hope Missie Patavine won't hab nuffin to do wid him.

Paris. [*Aside.*] Heaven forbid it! what means his presence ere her own home has had time to bid her welcome?

Cute. [*Aside.*] I don't believe dat I ought to tell him, kase he'll feel so bad. I spec dat I'll hab to, dough. [*Aloud.*] 'Twas he, Massa Paris, dat fotched Missie Patavine home, dey say—

Paris. [*Bewildered.*] He brought her home—it cannot be—you are jesting, Cute.

Cute. I wish I was, Massa Paris, but I ain't, kase I seen dem come in de carriage.

Paris. Oh, deception! can thee have so fair a deceiver to wear thy ignoble crown? Leave me, Cute. Speak not of me to her.

Cute. I'se sorry, Massa Paris, dat I told you, but don't tink so hard ob her, kase I knows dat its her fadder dat's all to blame—he is de cause ob it all—I knows dat de gal likes you. But I'll go, and hope to hab better news de next time. [*Exit* L.]

Paris. Likes me—yes, may be with the same attachment that the child holds it's toys—to be cast at each succeeding fancy. And yet, she is not wholly at fault, though she has consented to become the wife of Joel Mertloff; for the solicitations of a parent on the affections of a devoted child are not easily denied. No, Pedestin, I will not accuse you of the willful retrogression of thy vow; my own heart would feign tell me that I am yet thought of by thee; I would be less worthy to charge thee with fault—it is I who by mislead reason have been shadowing my own light with the fallacious claims of love. To have thee link thy life with that of mine, in defiance of thy parental will, would be robbing Justice to sanctify Crime. Oh, poverty! thou art a sacrilegeous grave to Love. Many is the heart thou hast broken. Oh, Pedestin—I free thee—I bless thee. May heaven be my valediction! [*Exit* R.]

SCENE III.—*A furnished apartment in the residence of Colonel Nortville.*

Enter PEDESTIN *and* CUTE, R.

Ped. Now, Cute, come tell me the truth. Have you not really seen Paris Desmer and told him that I am at home.

Cute. No, indeed, Missie Patavine, I didn't see him since—

Ped. Since when?

Cute. Dat long time dat I was gwine to de mill wid de grist and I met him huntin'.

Ped. [*Looking in his eyes.*] Now, Cute, I really can't believe that you have not seen Paris Desmer to-day. Now, look me straight in the face and say you did not.

Cute. [*Looks at her.*] Dar, now, I'se not seen him.

Ped. Cute, you don't know that I brought you a nice present from Baltimore.

Cute. No, I didn't, Missie Patavine.

Ped. O, yes, I have. [*Gets knife and pocket-book off the table.*]

Cute. [*Aside.*] I'se a notion to tell her dat I seen Massa Paris.

Ped. Now, Cute, these are yours, and here is five dollars for your pocket-book, so that it will not be empty. [*Gives them.*]

Cute. Lor' bless yo' soul, Missie Patavine, yous not gwine to gib me all dese tings.

Ped. Yes, Cute, they are all for you—I hope that you like them.

Cute. I does, Missie Patavine, but I'se not earned dem yet. You had better keep dem till I do. [*Offers them back.*]

Ped. No, no, Cute, they are yours—you have more than paid for them by your faithfulness long ago.

Cute. Tankee, missie; but long as I can do good for any one, I'se gwine to do it for you.

Ped. Thank you, Cute. [*Gets letter from her basket.*]

Cute. [*Aside.*] Oh, golly, [*Looking at knife.*] I'se got jus as nice a knife now as Massa Kurnel.

Ped. Cute, do you think that you could find Paris Desmer and give him this letter, without any one knowing anything about it.

Cute. I tinks I can. Massa Paris will be so glad to get it, kase I knows dat he—

Ped. That—what,?
Cute. Lubs you!
Ped. Loves me. [*Aside.*] Heaven grant that it is true. [*Aloud.*] You are jesting, Cute?
Cute. No, I'se not.
Ped. How do you know it?
Cute. Kase I do—and dat he's all de time wurrin' bout you. Oh, its easy tellin'—I'se often seed him go and set under de old tree dat you and him used to play by—and not go wid udder gals at all.
Ped. [*Feelingly.*] And this was all for me, you say.
Cute. Yes, Missie Patavine. He is so good to ebery one—not like dat Massa Joel Mertloff.
Ped. [*Aside.*] No, heaven forbid that he was. [*Aloud.*] Don't you like him, Cute?
Cute. No, I dosn't. I'se got no use for him, dar none ob de gemmen round him.
Ped. What does Paris say of him?
Cute. I doesn't know. Massa Paris keeps dat to hisself, do I suspeck dat his 'pinion is like mine. Kase he couldn't tink oderwise, and tink right.
Ped. Here, Cute, is the letter, give it to no one but him, I will await your return. [*Gives letter.*]
Cute. I will, Missie Patavine. I'll be off in tree flutters ob a possum's tail, and see Massa Paris. [*Aside.*] Won't he be glad to get dis letter, do'. Oh, golly! I feel like de ole time when I was de mail-bag before. [*Going, sees Col. Nortville, and hides letter.*]

Enter NORTVILLE, R.

Col. Well, Cute, I am sorry to part with you—I intend giving you away; but I think you will have a more lenient master than I have been.
Ped. Oh, father! you would not part with poor old Cute, who has given you a life time's service, and whose fidelity has never been wanting?

Cute. I'se berry sorry, Massa Kurnel, to leab you, for I isn't got many more days to lib no how. You'se always been a good massa to me. [*Appears sad.*]

Col. Yes, Cute, you have been faithful, that is the reason I feel sorry to part with you. I now give you to—

Ped. Oh, father! You won't part with him! See, the poor old man is already stooped with age—his hair is white by years of toil.

Col. If you are not satisfied, Pedestin, I will take him back again.

Ped. Then I am not.

Col. Yes, but I have not given him to you yet.

Ped. [*Delighted.*] To *me*, dear father!

Col. To you, and nobody else.

Ped. Oh, it is *me* then, that you intend giving Cute to?

Col. Yes—but you said that you would object to it.

Ped. No I won't, father, when it is to *me* you are going to give him. Will I, Cute?

Cute. No, indeed, Missie Patavine, and I'se *more* den satisfied.

Col. Well then, if you are 'both satisfied, I am. Now, Cute, you belong hereafter to Pedestin; you have but to obey her, and I think that you will not be sorry after all for the change.

Cute. I'se *sure* to do dat, massa Kurnel, and I won't be sorry eider.

Ped. No, Cute, you will have no cause to regret it.

Cute. I knows it, Missie Patavine.

Ped. You can go now Cute and saddle my pony, for I intend to go riding this morning. [*Aside to him.*] The letter, I mean.

Cute. [*To her.*] Yes, I knows dat. [*Aloud.*] I'll hab de pony ready, missie. [*Exit singing,* R.]

Ped. How am I to thank you, for all that you have done for me—not a wish—not a fancy that you have not gratified; and now you give me a prize I value more than all—Uncle Cute. [*They sit.*]

Col. Your love and obedience, Pedestin, have more than repaid me.

Ped. Yes, father, and I will always be so. I have no one to love and obey but you.

Col. [*Aside.*] I will soon test it. [*Aloud.*] Pedestin, I wish to speak to you on a matter that now absorbs my whole attention. My only wish now is to see you happy and well provided for.

Ped. I *am* happy, father, and wish for no other happiness than to live with and love you.

Col. Yes, my child, but you won't have me with you always, that is why I look forward to your marriage.

Ped. [*Much surprised.*] My marriage?

Col. Yes, daughter.

Ped. But I have never as yet given it a moment's thought.

Col. That is the reason, Pedestin, I speak of it now. I am getting infirm with age, and should I be taken away, I would wish to leave you to a husband's care, and one that would be faithful.

Ped. You are in good health, father—not suffering from any indisposition—and my prayer will be for its continuance.

Col. Bless you, my child. Pedestin, there is another reason that I would argue in favor of your early marriage. You know I am soon to leave for England, having been appointed arbitrator in the settlement of your uncle's estate. And as my stay may be for some months there, I would wish to see you married before I go. You have arrived at that age in which a protector, one that you can trust in all things, becomes indispensable. I know of none to whose charge I could better leave you than that of a husband's. You, who never had a mother's care, know not the anxiety, the uneasiness of mind that fall to a father's lot, to care for a daughter. If I am too persistant in my purpose, it is because your happiness and welfare are both involved. I have none but you, Pedestin; you were my early hope—now be the comfort of my declining years—and a father's blessing will be yours.

Ped. I thought not but to please your slightest wish. I know of no privation, no toil—no matter how laborious or self-denying that I am not willing to endure for you. But when you summon my affection, my love for he whom I know naught of, I must deny thee.

Col. But my daughter, you know not who I mean. Why speak so resolutely, it may be that his name will meet with the approval of your heart ere my tongue has fully told it.

Ped. If it is your wish I will hear it, father.

Col. Then, my dear Pedestin, I will tell you it, and one whose wealth and station calls forth envy from many. His age and appearance are both in keeping with his manly bearing—Joel Mertloff.

Ped. [*Starts.*] Joel Mertloff! Can you be serious, father?

Col. Yes, I am. Why should I not; he is worthy of the best lady in the country.

Ped. Then father, I am sorry that you have encouraged this in thought, for it can never be.

Col. Never be! but you are forgetting his integrity—his high position, and his great wealth.

Ped. I am forgetting nothing, father, for sooner would I be free—and beg in the tattered garbs of poverty, than be a *slave* in chains of gold!

Col. Then if such is your resolve, Pedestin, it behooves me to tell you the truth, that I would wish to keep from you. Know then, that I am bankrupt, and indebted most to him.

Ped. [*Startled.*] You——bankrupt!

Col. Yes daughter, I am. My estate is mortgaged, and were I pushed by my creditors, I would not own a dollar. Joel Mertloff is my sole one.

Ped. [*Aside.*] And it could not be to a worse one. [*Aloud.*] Oh, father, would that this could be averted, for your sake. I care not for myself; life is all before me; but you, who has been so kind a father to me, I will unceasingly toil—labor to support you—beg, were it necessary; but ask me not to become the wife of Joel Mertloff.

Col. Then you close the only means of escape that is left us from beggary—your marriage with him is the last and only resource. I will give you until to-morrow to decide, and let us not be cast upon the world penniless. [*Going.*] [*Aside.*] I think that will have the desired effect. [*Exit* L.]

Ped. 'Till to-morrow to decide between ignominious slavery and poverty. The preference is momentious for one's life. One adds reproach by silence, and mockery by smiles; in the other, there is hope, that gives cheer in the most trying moments. But can I see my father, worn by care, whose hair is whi'ened by the sorrows of time, become a beggar—an outcast—he that has lavished luxury and wealth upon me; never yet denied me aught? No, I cannot see him suffer—I am not ungrateful—I am his daughter. [*Weeps.*]

Enter Rose Merview, L.

Rose. Why, my dear Pedestin, you have been crying. What in the world could have affected your gentle heart—you look so pale, too—won't you tell me, dear? [*Sits.*]

Ped. I am grieved to hear of father leaving so soon for England, and be absent so long.

Rose. Why—is he going so soon as that? I thought he would not leave for a month yet.

Red. Yes, he will leave immediately.

Rose. But why take it so much to heart, dear cousin? He certainly will not be very long absent—and besides, you have been so long away from home that you will find much enjoyment in reviewing your early haunts and pass-times, that will in a great degree obviate the tediousness that would follow. Now, be cheerful, and imagine that he—[*Laughs.*] you know who I mean—was looking at you. I warrant that you would look sweet then. Ah! cousin.

Ped. Those days are past, Rose,—they were life's happiest hours.

Rose. Yes, and just as happy ones to come.

Ped. [*Aside.*] I hope so.

Rose. But why don't you take pattern after me, cousin. For my part I would not care if all the young men in the country were off ballooning and never returned, you would not catch me studying astronomy—no indeed—I would not look at the stars for a month after.

Ped. Yes, cousin, I wish I was as free from care as you are. Time makes no change in you—the same free, wild Rose.

Rose. Yes, and I am going to be. If every one was like me there would be no inquests held on victims of blighted love that are now becoming so epidemic. I believe in every one loving themselves best. But then, if one has a superfluous quantity of it, let them divide it equally among their fellow creatures serving one and all alike.

Ped. [*Laughing.*] Why, what a philanthropist you are becoming, Rose.

Rose. Oh, yes. I am quite a prodigy, I assure you.

Ped. Cousin, you often promised me that you would tell me all about that early love you had for a certain young man, and I have yet to learn his name, too.

Rose. I will tell you now, providing you say nothing about it.

Ped. I will readily promise that.

Rose. I was engaged to a very nice young man at the early age of sixteen. He was four years older than myself. We were school-mates, and raised, you might say, beneath the same roof. His father was a sea captain, and on his last voyage to China died there. Walter, my intended, went after his father, and on his return home, one year after, he broke off the engagement, apparently without any cause at the time; but since, I heard that it was occasioned by some family troubles. His people moved from our town two years previous, and I never heard definitely of them since, and not at all of him. He was the noblest of his sex—and though I have not seen him in four long years, I am still susceptible to the belief that I will.

Ped. I hope that you will—but you forgot to tell me his name.

Rose. Walter Benson.

Ped. I don't remember of ever having heard the name.

Rose. I dare say not. But did I tell you the news I heard in the village.

Ped. No—what is it?

Rose. Why, I heard that Paris Desmer is going to the gold regions.

Ped. What gold regions?

Rose. The gold regions in California, I suppose.

Ped. [*Starts.*] Oh, cousin, are you not jesting? He would not leave the country without seeing me, when he knows that I am at home.

Rose. How can he see you, when your father forbids his entering the house?

Ped. Oh, I must see him—I would have him know all, and not think that I ever deceived him.

Rose. All what, cousin? I fear you have some secret of no pleasing nature, that you would keep from me—why not confide in me?—but I will not press you more.

Ped. I will tell you all some other time. I do not wish to cause you unnecessary solicitude now, for it would be of no avail.

Rose. As you wish, dear cousin; but be more cheerful, you are too sensitive—your kind heart is too open and too apt to magnify trifles, for your bodily comfort. But, come, let us take a walk in the garden, and, if I mistake not, the morning zephyrs will lure that ill-meaning spirit away.

Ped. I look for Cute's return from the village every moment—I sent him there with a letter to—

Rose. To Paris Desmer. [*Laughs.*] O, you rogue, before an hour, you will be as happy as a lark.

[*Exit* L.]

Enter COL. NORTVILLE *and* JOEL MERTLOFF.

Col. Leave that to me Joel, I have already brought a little artifice to my aid and I think from present prospects that it will work admirably.

Joel. Yes, that's it, Colonel, one ounce of strategy is worth a regiment of bayonets. But as long as that worthless skulking cur, Paris Desmer, stays in the neighborhood I fear that he will revert her attention.

Col. Why, he is gone—gone to the gold regions, I was told to-day by those who know.

Joel. [*Aside.*] I wish it was to the devil. [*Aloud.*] Gone there, ah!

Col. Yes, he made his farewell bow to the villagers last evening. I never knew that Pedestin had any particular liking for this fellow, but women are so devilish odd that there is no accounting for their fancy.

Joel. They are, indeed, a pack of insolvable mysteries, Colonel, every one of them. I was aware of Pedestin liking this Desmer; but, as love in the young is but a fancied idea, it can easily be frightened out. However, I will leave that to you.

Col. Well you may, I have things now pretty much as I wish them—the greatest obstacles are surmounted.

Joel. Does she know of your going to England, Colonel?

Col. Yes, I so informed her, but said nothing in regard to the estate my Uncle left me, and I would warn you on that point, also.

Joel. Ha, ha, a little more device, Colonel; there is nothing like it.

Col. It takes persistance in an affair of this kind. I have never undertaken anything that I did not accomplish. I have set my heart on this marriage, and unless I am greatly astray I will bring it to a successful issue. What think you, Joel?

Joel. I hope so, Colonel.

Col. Joel, as much as I dote on her, and were she to marry any worthless fellow, hang me if would not disinherit her—cut her off without a dollar. It is well for you that I hold you in such high favor.

Joel. Thank you, Colonel, for that. I suppose it is not necessary for me to make any suggestions now as to preparations for our nuptials.

Col. No, not now. That is like paying the fiddler before the dance. But what say you if you stop in and see her. Speak not of your marriage to her—to-day, at all events.

Joel. As you wish Colonel, [*going*] I will see you presently. [*Aside.*] Now to feast my eyes upon her beauty. [*Exit* L.]

Col. What better man could she expect to get than he is. He is rich, young, noble looking, and certainly of good parentage. Hang me if I can see what is getting into the marriageable daughters now days. Their fancy is as peculiar as the fool who wanted to marry his own mother [*Cute opens door in* c., *and is about to come in, letter in hand, sees Colonel Nortville, stands at door and listens.*] Ha, ha, I have the best of it so far. Telling her that I was bankrupt will have more influence to induce her to marry [*Cute puts his head inside of door.*] Joel Mertloff than all other stories I could coin. By to-morrow I will have the gentle yes from her—I will take no other answer. I am better pleased than a thousand dollars to hear of that scamping fellow, Desmer, leaving the country, [*Cute shows the audience letter*] and if he never returns until I bid him welcome, this locality will be free from his presence for a while. [*Exit* R.]

Enter CUTE.

Cute. Golly, wouldn't Massa Kurnel gib my ear a pullin' if he ketched me hecar'n on him. Dar is some flicker in de wind when he talks dat way 'bout Miss Patavine. I guess dat he's kind o' 'stakin if he tinks dat she's gwine to marry Massa Mertloff. Not as long as dis ere chile' knows hisself, bankruckery or no bankrukery, kase I knows it as well as Massa Kurnel. I'se got de letter here for Miss Patavine, and Massa Paris is not gone yet. He is gwine to see her to-morrow night. [*Looks at the letter.*] Jus de same marks dat was on dem before. Oh, I'll bet dat dar is lots of lub in dat letter. 'Tis de white folks dat can talk de lub, kase dey larn it in de books. [*Exit* R, *singing.*]

SCENE IV.—*Plain Room.*

Enter CUTE *and* ROSE.

Rose. Well, then, what is the reason, Cute, that the young gentlemen, as you are pleased to term them, don't like me?

Cute. I'se don't know Missie Rose, 'less 'tis—

Rose. Unless what, Cute?

Cute. Dat dey tink you talk too much, Missie Rose.

Rose. Me talk too much, you rascal. [*Going for him; Cute backing away.*] How dare have you the impudence to say that I talk too much?

Cute. No, I mean dem oder fellers, Missie Rose, dat said it. [*Aside.*] Oh, laws, I wouldn't ker about her mysef.

Rose. You say that again and I will—

Cute. Yes, I knows you would.

Rose. What is my tongue for but to use it?

Cute. Yes, I knows dat. [*Aside.*] You does, and your hands sometimes, too.

Rose. It is of little difference whether the young men fancy my talking or not. You tell them so for me.

Cute. [*Aside.*] No, I'se gwine to tell dem nothing. [*Aloud.*] 'Twas dem dat said it, Missie Rose. I was only tellin' it ober.

Rose. Oh, well, if that is it, I will forgive. But, now, tell me what Harry Ward said about me, and I will give you a nice present.

Cute. Oh, yes, dat one you didn't gib me, and was gwin' to gib me last Christmas.

Rose. Yes, that one.

Cute. I'se 'fraid dat you will forgit it as you did dat one, Missie Rose.

Rose. Oh, no, you can remind me of it, Cute.

Cute. Well, but my new rules is for work like dis is git paid in 'vance, den you won't forgot it.

Rose. Pay in advance, eh? Why, Cute, you are really up to the times.

Cute. I'd rather have a dollar, if it is de same to you, Missie Rose.

Rose. Why, I didn't say dimes, but then I believe I have a little change [*takes out coppers*] about me.

Cute. [*Aside.*] Yes, 'tis little too.

Rose. There, I hope that will satisfy you.
Cute. Yes, to look at, but I can't buy nuffin wid dem, dey are, [*looking at them*] are—
Rose. They are pennies, what we use East for change.
Cute. Yes, I taught dat dey come from dar.
Rose. Well, now, tell me what Harry said.
Cute. Oh, yes. Well, he said dat you war—
Rose. What?
Cute. [*Look off* L.] Oh, here comes Massa Kurnel, and I must make mysef skarce 'bout dis time.
Rose. But, tell me, what did he say, Cute.
Cute. [*Going.*] Dat you was too old. [*Exit* R.]
Rose. I, too old. Well, what contemptible, unprincipled bigots men are—big and little, old and young—to call me old, and I have not seen my twenty-first year yet—

Enters COL. NORTVILLE, L.

they are all a chip of the one block.
Col. Good morning, Cousin Rose. What is it that now disturbs the tranquility of your peacable mind. Some new breakers, eh?
Rose. Breakers, yes. You men are a clog to every woman's happiness.
Col. Me?
Rose. No, not you, now, Uncle. You have passed that age. You were once a man.
Col. [*Aside.*] Hang me if that ain't complimentary—I was "once a man"—[*Aloud.*] And what am I now, Cousin Rose?
Rose. [*Coaxingly.*] A nice, quiet, old gentleman, Uncle.
Col. [*Aside.*] That's an improvement, but still not exactly the thing. [*Aloud.*] I am not so very old, Cousin Rose.
Rose. No, Uncle, you are not quite eighty, I believe.

Col. Eighty! Why, bless you, I have not seen fifty yet. I was just twenty years old when you were born. I remember the night well. So that brings you close on to thirty.

Rose· Uncle, what an unfeeling wretch you are. Me thirty. Not for nine years yet. [*Going, and stands on his toes.*] I will be even with you yet for—

Col. Oh! my toes, my toes—

Rose. Don't wear such tight boots, uncle. [*Exit* R.]

Col. I had better wear iron ones when your corporation feet are around. Whoever has the fortune of getting her will get a tartar. Her small fortune is unsufficient to keep up and I am the sufferer. Now, for Pedestin and her yes. It must be seriously comtemplated by her, for she has not left her room to-day.

Enter JOEL MERTLOFF, L.

Joel. Good-evening, colonel, I come for your company in that drive you promised to take with me this evening.

Col. Oh, yes, I'd quite forgotten it, Joel.

Joel. How is Miss Pedestin—anything demonstrative?

Col. No—not as yet. Really, I have not seen her to-day—she has kept her room.

Joel. She is inclined to be self-willed, colonel!

Col. Not to control her. I was on the point of calling on her when you came in. If you will spare me for a few moments, I will see her. [*Exit both,* L.]

Enter PEDESTIN, R., *looking pale.*

Ped. The hour is already at hand when I am to give my father an answer. May heaven direct me in giving it; I cannot see my good father, now in his declining years, deprived of a home—cast upon the charity of a merciless world. Yet—death is preferable—than to be the wife of Joel Mertloff.

Enter CUTE, L.

Cute. Missie Patavine, you has been crying—I hope dat you isn't sick.
Ped. Cute, I have good cause to shed tears.
Cute. Can't I do nuffin for you, Missie Patavine? Is dar been any one saying something to you?
Ped. No, Cute—not that, but far worse. I will tell you, for I know I can trust you.
Cute. Yes, missie, you can dat—for I'll neber deseebe, dough I is a poor ole nigger.
Ped. You are faithful. My father wants me to marry Joel Mertloff, for, in so-doing, I will save him from bankruptcy—beggary—for he is now on the verge of both.
Cute. I tells you, Missie Patavine, don't marry him, kase I knows better dan dat—'tis all smoke, kase I knows it—don't marry him, 'twould wurry poor Massa Paris. [*Much moved.*]
Ped. What do you mean by your knowing better?
Cute. I'se heard Massa Kurnel talking to hissef—don't marry him, Missie Patavine, kase dar is no bankruckery at all.
Ped. No—bankruptcy!
Cute. No, dar isn't.
Ped. I believe you, Cute, your honesty is expressive in every word. O, heaven, I thank thee for my deliverance—I now comprehend all—my eyes are open to the deception that would have deprived me of life and liberty. Still more galling is the thought that my own father would be the extortioner. [*Steps heard coming.*] Here comes my father—leave, Cute, I would not have him see you here now.
Cute. I'se gwine, Missie Patavine, but don't marry him, kase dar is no bankruckery at all. [*Exit,* R.]

Enter COLONEL NORTVILLE, L.

Col. My dear daughter, I was becoming uneasy at your absence, all day. I hope you are not unwell.

Ped. No, father, not that.

Col. Ah! I see you think that your non-appearance is in keeping with the sad news of yesterday. You are right, daughter, it is.

Ped. Yes, father, such was my motive.

Col. I hope, Pedestin, that you have fully decided.

Ped. I have.

Col. To marry him, of course.

Ped. Who?

Col. Joel Mertloff—who else?

Ped. Father—Joel Mertloff, I can not and—will not marry.

Col. [*Surprised.*] What, daughter, not to save your father from ruin and disgrace.

Ped. Father, I will do anything that a child can do to save a parent. I will deny myself—toil—drudge—beg—for you; but to marry Joel Mertloff, before heaven, do I attest that I never will!

Col. Listen, Pedestin, you have had your choice, and this is your decision. Now, I will have mine and I will act accordingly. Not a dollar of mine will you receive until you consent to marry Joel Mertloff, and should that not be before my death, I will disinherit you, you disobedient, ungrateful hussy. This is your thanks for all I have done for you. Mark me—you shall be the sufferer. [*Exit*, R. *Pedestin weeps.*]

Ped. It is all passed now, and I trust to heaven that it is for the better. His own words tell me that it was a snare to rob me of what earth cannot restore—its wealth can never buy my love and my honor—for, to become the wife of Joel Mertloff, would be a stigma on both. [*Exit.* L.]

Scene IV.—*A Garden; moon seen through the trees.*

Enter Paris Desmer, l.

Paris. Her letter says that she would meet me here at nine, [*Looks at his watch.*] it wants but five minutes of the time. Why does she ask this meeting, when every tongue proclaim the day of her marriage with another? There can be but one alternative—the dreams of youth are no longer suggestive of reality. It would be madness to persist in them longer—baseness in me, to link her with my poverty—no! no! the thought is too preposterous. It would be plucking the rose, bathed in bloom, to be witness of its death.

Enter Pedestin, r.

Ped. Oh, Paris, you are here—thank you for this. [*She rushes into his arms.*]

Paris. I came at your request, dear Pedestin.

Ped. Oh, dear Paris, forgive me if I have acted wrong in bringing you here; but I could not help it —I heard that you were about to leave the country. I could not suffer you to go without first seeing you.

Paris. Why should I stay?—poverty is all that seem to greet me here—our vows of love have long since ceased—they were but the idle dreams of our young hearts—wanting better judgment, for we were both, then, in child-like innocence. But that is all now passed—we have grown in years, and should exercise more considerate discrimination; in the future, let our motives be governed by reason, for our paths in life will be far apart. It is the same love that entered my heart for you when a boy that now counsels this; it has grown too deep—too holy—too infinite— to have you linked with my misfortune—I alone can suffer my privations—but to have you share them—no—never!

Ped. [*Aside.*] You are too noble.

Paris. But let me hope that in your new condition you will become happy—reconciled to heaven's will.

Ped. [*Starts.*] What means that new condition you speak of?

Paris. Is it not on every tongue that is able to speak your name?

Ped. I can not understand you, Paris.

Paris. Would you be married—and yet—not know it—when the rumor is afloat that you soon will—

Ped. Me—no—'tis impossible—that rumor is false—to whom does it say?

Paris. To Joel Mertloff.

Ped. It is a falsehood—a malicious and unmitigated falsehood! Never have I, in word or act, given encouragement to his suit—and I will affirm—that I never will. It is true he accompanied me home from school. but that was the express wish of my father, and I could not reasonably object to it. Paris, think not for an instant that my love for you has undergone any change, for it has not—I would have you know me as I am. Could you but read my lacerated heart, it would reveal you all. What think you, when a father would become identical with a scheme to rob his own child of heaven's holiest gift; to destroy that love it gave as a blessing, to be free, holy and undefiled; to cast an odium upon it—become instrumental in the annihilation of its sanctity?

Paris. Is it possible that you accuse your father of this?

Ped. Such is my fear that he is so disposed. Blame me not if I lose faith in all, when he whose blood runs in my veins would barter his own child.

Paris. Be more hopeful, Pedestin: the future will yet bestow on you the brightest hues of its glory.

Ped. I have one hope left me still, and that is you, Paris. Do not turn away from me—I would be with you—beggar—outcast—all that you might be. [*Falls in his arms weeping.*]

Paris. This must not—cannot be—my strength is failing me. Pedestin, my angel, my love, [*Kisses her.*] may heaven care thee until we meet there. [*Going.*]

Ped. Oh! Paris, lover, you will not leave me—

Paris. No, my heart ever remains with you.
[*Exit* L.]

Ped. Paris—lover—[*Starts after him.*] you will not leave me. Oh! God, he is gone—he is gone, and life is worthless without him. [*Sinks weeping. Quick fall of curtain.*]

END OF ACT I.

ACT II.

SCENE I.—*Same as Scene III, Act I. Pedestin seated at table, reading; Rose drawing.*

Ped. [*Putting down paper.*] I cannot read; my sight wanders over its pages and discerns nothing. I fear I will never see him again.

Rose. Cousin, I would exhort you to hope more. The vexatious taunts that every bereaved heart is heir to should not be indulged in. Be more inflexible, then, I'll warrant you more happiness.

Ped. [*Aside.*] Advice is easier given than taken. [*Aloud.*] It is now two months, and yet no tidings come from him. He may be dead!

Rose. Dead? No—why—if you keep in that way you will soon become an anatomist of mortality.

Ped. Even his mother does not hear from him, which is more strange, and she is too, apprehensive of his safety.

Rose. There is uncle, who has been absent almost as long, and he has written but once—and that was not to us.

Ped. Father was in poor health when he wrote: that may have prevented him from writing since.

Rose. And, if Paris went to the gold regions, as the report said, he would not be apt to write until he got there—and that will take him some months; for, in that part of Uncle Sam's dominion, they don't travel by lightning express trains—no—indeed.

Ped. I did not think of that, cousin.

Rose. As to uncle not writing, that is quite easily solved. You know he was much displeased on account of your refusal to marry that obtrusive jack-a-napes, Joel Mertloff, Esq.

Ped I didn't think he would remember that when abroad.

Rose. Men will remember anything. For my part, I have but little faith in any of the amiable creatures. There is not one of them that has not as many faces as a dodecagon, and a color for each. No man can be trusted until he is a father—that is a grandfather—and then some of them are not reliable.

Ped. I hope, dear cousin, you don't class all men alike.

Rose. Oh, no—once in a while you will meet one, whose insipidness is a passport to morality.

Ped. You are too severe, cousin. I do wish Cute would return—I sent him to the village for the mail.

Enter CUTE, R.

Cute. Missie Patavine, I'se been to de village and

dar ain't no letters dar. De letter man looked in all de holes and couldn't find one for you. I met Massa Mertloff comin' dis way, I speck dat he am comin' hyar.

Ped. Joel Mertloff coming here again?

Rose. I suppose to show us his pugnacious countenance, which is equal to a dose of physic.

Cute. Missie Patavine, I'se agwine to stay close by, and if he say anyting dat's gruby, I'll club him like I would a snake.

Rose. And with your permission, cousin, I will withdraw for a few moments. [*Exit* L.]

Cute. I hears him comin', so I'll stow mysef way byar. [*Hides back of wing* L.]

Ped. There is no alternative for me but to see him. I would avoid the meeting, though I fear him not.

Enter JOEL MERTLOFF, R.

Joel. Ah! Miss Nortville, this is an unlooked-for pleasure. May I indulge in the belief that I do not intrude?

Ped. Mr. Mertloff, I am not disposed to deny any one who desires an interview, much less a friend of my father.

Joel. Thank you for the honor, Miss Nortville. [*Aside.*] That is the reason you tolerate me, I suppose. [*Aloud.*] Have you heard of late from your father?

Ped. No sir—not for some weeks.

Joel. You are aware that that he was in very poor health on his arrival in London.

Ped. Yes—it was from there he wrote.

Joel. [*Aside.*] 'Tis well you know no more. [*Aloud.*] Miss Nortville, I cannot forbear the temptation of broaching to you again the subject of our last interview. I fear that I was too imperious at the time; now, with your permission, I would exonerate myself.

Ped. That, sir, is as you wish it.

Joel. I would wish you to believe that it never was my intention to be instrumental in the restrainment of your better feelings, for, I believe not in the repression of one's choice. Love should never become a sacrifice on the altar of hymen. I must confess that I was—and I am as yet—zealous in the marriage your father was so anxious to bring about; I hoped to win your affections, your love, which I prize above all, and until I do, I would lay no claim to your hand; for, it would be but to smite my own conscience. Let me hope that the change will come, if it has not already, and the long-cherished attachment I have ever entertained for you will be the realization of my fond hopes. [*Advances to her.*] Here let me pledge you my sincerity, my love, and seal it with a—[*Tries to kiss her.*]

Ped. Back, ruffian! [*They tussle.*] Help—help: [*Cute appears from behind scene—dashes Mertloff off—catches Pedestin, who has fainted, and sits her in chair.*]

Cute. How dare you lay your flippers on dis lady! You is no man—no gemman—to do it. I'll grub you like a puppy, if you dare tink ob dat again.

Joel. You black, infernal imp—how dare you interrupt a gentleman! I'll punish your impudence as it deserves. [*Draws a pistol, is about to fire at Cute, Pedestin recovers.*]

Ped. Oh! don't shoot him, I pray you—he is not to blame—spare his life for my sake!

Cute. Don't be skeer, Missie Patavine, kase dar is no danger—he's not courage to shoot—I'se not 'larmed ob his pistol.

Joel. For your sake, I will spare his life. [*Aside.*] For it is not worth taking. [*Aloud.*] Miss Nortville, I wish you a good day, and I hope this will not be thought of seriously. [*Going.*] [*Aside.*] Before heaven, I swear that you will yet be my wife, or feel the weight of my vengeance. [*Exit* R.]

Cute. I hopes dat you is not hurt any, is you?
Ped. No, Cute, not at all. I am thankful for your aid—you will be better rewarded hereafter.
Cute. Dat's nuffin, Missie Patavine, I'se only glad dat I was dar.
Ped. I could not believe he possessed a heart so vicious, so basely inclined. [*Exit* L.]
Cute. I knew dat a long time ago. He has de blackest heart for a white-face man dat I eber seen. I'd jus like to cook his goose for 'bout five minits, and he wouldn't keer 'bout skeerin' any more ladies for one monf. [*Exit* R.]

Enter LAWYER MASON *and* ROSE.

Mason. Miss Merview, I would wish you to break the news to her, and as gently as possible. Her father died in London, on the 14th—three weeks tomorrow. His will, I must say, seems to be a little misty to me, and no less astonishing. His wealth, too, has been greatly increased by the large estate he became heir to, through the death of his uncle.
Rose. [*Anxiously.*] Does not the will give Cousin Pedestin his entire wealth, Mr. Mason?
Mason. Under certain stipulations, it does.
Rose. Stipulations! I don't exactly understand that term. Stipulations—in a will?
Mason. They are these: She becomes heir to her father's wealth—first, if his son George, who was stolen by some unknown parties, when an infant, is never recovered; and secondly, if she consents to become the wife of Mr. Joel Mertloff.
Rose. That she never will be, not for the wealth of the Rothchilds.
Mason. Then she is cut off with a small homestead, the will giving his nephews, Charles, Augustus, Herbert and Spencer Kimbell, a fortune of a million, and ten thousand dollars to a sister, living in Canada.

Rose. Yes, Aunt Martha.

Mason. I will call again in a few days, Miss Merview, and, in the mean time break the news to your cousin. Give her my sympathy and condolence. I would wish her to give this due consideration before I take any final action. [*Exit* R.]

Rose. Well, if that ain't enough to put any one in a perfect commotion, to hear of an unfeeling old renegade father leaving his own child almost penniless, because she would not marry one of the most consumate scamps that ever escaped the gallows. Only another illustration of the *noble* qualites that profusely augments masculine gender. Oh, man, your sins are more numerous than the blades of grass— a deluge of tears would not wipe them out. [*Exit* L.]

SCENE II.—*A set cottage, door,* R *flat.*

Enter CUTE, L, *with a letter.*

Cute. Missie Patavine send me down hyar wid a letter to Missus Desmer, Massa Paris' moder. I hope dat sh's to home, for dis 'bout bery 'portant business, I'm sure, and sometin' 'bout Massa Paris, too. De ole' lady, I spec, is snoosin', kase I sees no smoke in de chimney. [*Knocks at door.*] Missus Desmer, I hears her movin', she's home.

Enter MRS. DESMER, *from cottage.*

Mrs. D. Oh, it's you, Cute, and the last one I was looking for to-day.

Cute. Yes, Missus Desmer, I likes alway to come and see you, when I hab good news to tell you.

Mrs. D. You have good news to tell me, then. What is it, cute?

Cute. Missie Patavine would like for you to come ober and see her. We's gwine norf in a few days, and she wants to see you 'fore we goes. Hyar is a letter dat she gab me for you. 'Twill tell you all 'bout Massa Kurnel dyin', and ebery ing. [*Gives letter.*]

Mrs. D. It is true, then, that he is dead. [*Opens letter and looks over it.*]

Cute. Yes, and I tinks dat he's gone to no good place, needer.

Mrs. D. Well, Cute, you can tell Miss Pedestin that I will be happy to comply with her request.

Cute. Yes, I will, Missus Desmer. [*Exit* L, *singing.*]

Mrs. D. Poor child. She inquires particularly after Paris, and hopes that his silence is not occasioned by any accident. She loves him, and he idolizes her. May heaven grant that their devoted hearts will be yet united. She little dreams of the mystery that caused her to be raised Pedestin Nortville instead of Angeline Desmer. Oh, thank God that the time may soon come that she will know her mother. I have yet Mrs. Nortville's dying confession of the death of her infant daughter, and the particulars attending the same. Now, as he, whose implacable obstinacy would ever rule all, has passed away, I look with joy to the hour that Paris will, by his own right, become the lawful heir. [*Exit door.*]

Enter WALTER BRUCE, L.

Bruce. [*Looks at the cottage.*] I believe that this is the cottage of Paris Desmer. I would see his mother were she at home—at all events I will knock and see—for the life of him whom she loves with the tender affection of a mother's heart—depends on me seeing her. Joel Mertloff, in his thirst for blood, now hankers for the life of her son. It is but a few moments ago that I parted with him. He was then coming here to ask the poor mother of her son's whereabouts, that he might follow him up with his murderous intent and take his life, for what he denominates vengance. But I will foil you here, Mertloff, and will until I see you swinging from the gallows. [*Knocks at the door.*] Ho, Mrs. Desmer.

Re-enter MRS. DESMER.

Mrs. D. Was it you that called, sir?

Bruce. Yes, madam, it was. I have a few words I wish to say to you. They are of the utmost importance, for the life of him you hold as dear as your own, depends on them.

Mrs. D. [*Excitedly.*] Speak, sir, I pray you, is he—I mean my son, Paris—in danger?

Bruce. No, madam, not yet, but will be unless you'll be advised.

Mrs. D. Proceed, sir, I will hear.

Bruce. There is a certain person who has conspired against his life, and will, perhaps to-day, make inquiry of you as to his whereabout. Make him none the wiser of your knowledge.

Mrs. D. Oh, heaven. Who could harbor malice against he who never said aught to any one?

Bruce. One who would do so against a saint.

Mrs. D. Such he must be.

Bruce. Madam, I have told you this much at my own risk. Should suspicion arise—

Mrs. D. I will show my thanks for your merited kindness by keeping suspicion down.

Bruce. Then your son's life will be saved, and his would-be-assassin baffled, madam. Good day. I know not how soon you may have another visitor. [*Exit* L.]

Mrs. D. And I will go in-doors and not come out, no matter who calls. [*Going.*] Oh, thank heaven that Paris is in no danger. [*Exit door.*]

Scene III.—*Same as Scene I, Act II.*

Enter Mr. Mason *and* Pedestin.

Mason. It does not meet with my approval, Miss Nortville, and knowing your father so well, it surprises me more. I am powerless to act only as the will stipulates. Yet, I will favor you all I possibly can, for I am sensible of its injustice.

Ped. Thank you, Mr. Mason.

Mason. You have no knowledge of the facts connected with your brother's abduction?

Ped. No, sir, only what I heard others say.

Mason. I do not quite understand how it occurred. It was prior to my acquaintance with your family. You and your brother were of the same age, I believe.

Ped. Yet, sir, we were born twins. He was but six months old when he was stolen, and, as many supposed, by some wandering gipsies, that infested the neighborhood at the time. Father made vigilant search for him, and offered large rewards, but all to no purpose. One year after my mother died, broken hearted, on account of it.

Mason. It is, indeed, sad enough.

Ped. The loss of my brother made father, at times, surly toward me. I often heard him say that he wished I were taken instead of him.

Mason. [*Moved.*] No doubt that it did. I will take no action for the present, Miss Nortville. The means you require to make this intended tour North, you speak of, I will place in the bank, subject to your order, and should you determine otherwise than the present, apprise me of it.

Ped. No, Mr. Mason, my mind is resolute. To become the wife of Joel Mertloff I never will. I spurn the thought as I would a viper.

Mason. [*Aside.*] Neither do I blame you. [*Aloud.*]

I hope that it is all for the best, Miss Nortville. I will bid you good-day.

Ped. Good-day, Mr. Mason. I am thankful for your kindness. [*Exit Mason,* R.]

Enter ROSE L.

Rose. Dear Pedestin, do you really intend taking this trip North immediately?

Ped. Yes, cousin, I do.

Rose. So unexpectedly. Why not wait a few days. What is the object of going so soon?

Ped. Can't you guess, cousin?

Rose. I have been trying to, but I am as much in the dark as ever.

Ped. Oh, cousin. If you possessed my heart for one minute it would tell you with a thousand tongues.

Rose. [*Thoughtfully.*] Your heart—oh, yes, I have it now. Why, noble cousin, you are a worthy symbol of woman's sincerity—would risk all—would sacrifice all—for the one you love.

Ped. You do not blame me, then, for going, Rose.

Rose. Blame you?—no—I will go with you and help you to find him.

Ped. Thank you, dear cousin, I wished your company, but I was afraid to ask it.

Rose. Now you have it without asking. I will go and make the necessary arrangements. [*Exit,* R.]

Enter CUTE, *in haste,* L., *with a band-box tied by a rope.*

Cute. I'se got all de trunks packed and de band-boxes, Missie Patavine, I'se gwine to take dis ere one 'long to tote my tings in; I'sen't got so many, so dat dis will do. [*Sits it on stage and unties rope.*] I speck dat I can take Massa Kurnel's coat dat is hangin' up in de garret. [*Opens band-box, takes out stocking, shirt, vest, collars, and a large pistol.*] I'se gwine to take dis 'long to cook Massa Mertloff's goose, if I sees him up dar. [*Shows audience pistol.*] You sees I'se takin' 'long jus what I needs on de road.

Ped. [*Laughing.*] You have a great idea of traveling, Cute.

Cute. Yes, I hab dat—I'se been dar 'fore now. Is we gwine to all de big towns up dar, whar all de bad people lib and de rogues, too?

Ped. Yes, Cute, we will visit them all.

Cute. And Chicago, too?

Ped. Yes, we take it in.

Cute. I'se 'fraid dat it will take us in. I'se gwine to keep mighty shy ob dat place.

Ped. Leave that band-box here, I'll give you a valise to put your clothes in—and that coat you speak of, for you will have a traveling suit.

Cute. Thankee, Missie Patavine. [*Aside.*] Oh, golly, I'se gwine to be no common nig, I tells you.

Ped. Put everything in readiness, we will leave to-morrow evening.

Cute. Is we going by de cars or by de boats, Missie Patavine?

Ped. By both, Cute.

Cute. [*Aside.*] I won't sleep to-night from tinkin' ob de good time I'se gwine to hab.

[*Exit with band-box, singing,* L.]

Ped. I have yet to see Mrs. Desmer—she sends me a note, so blotted that I can hardly read it, saying that her poor health will prevent her from calling to-day, but will to-morrow. She further adds that Paris parting from me was like parting his life; but rather than have me share his distress, he would see me another's.

Re-enter CUTE, *with a cane and a stove-pipe hat.*

Cute. Missie Patavine, has you any objection if I

takes dis 'ere walking-stick and dis hat ob Massa 'long? I speck dat I'll hab use for dem, too.

Ped. [*Laughing.*] No, Cute, take them if you wish. [*Exit.* L.]

Cute. [*Puts on hat, walks across stage, takes pistol from pocket.*] I'se all right now for de road, for I'se gwine to cook Massa Mertloff's goose, if I eber sees him up dar. [*Exit* L.]

Scene IV.—*A Street.*

Enter Joel Mertloff *and* Walter Bruce, L.

Joel. You are becoming as whimsical as a grandmother of eighty. You have but one time to die, and what's the odds whether it is this year or next, as long as you don't die with a hemp neck-tie furnished at the expense of the State.

Bruce. So, you wouldn't wish then to die in that improved style, Joel.

Joel. No, no; any other death in preference to an elevated one—my neck was never intended to stretch hemp.

Bruce. [*Aside.*] Time will tell.

Joel. A man who dies on the gollows, Bruce, not only disgraces his own name, but that of every one bearing it. Enough of this—now to business.

Bruce. Proceed, I am all ears.

Joel. The parties of whom I speak are coming here to take passage up the river, I don't know how high up; but it matters little, for we must trap them in the first convenient place. This miss is very rich, her father leaving her his entire wealth, provided she marries me—and that, she has seen fit to kick against. This scamping fellow, Paris Desmer, that I spoke to you about, she is in love with, and from what I hear, is making this trip north in hope of

finding him. She is also accompanied by her cousin, Rose Merview, and a servant—
Bruce. [*Starts.*] Rose Merview—
Joel. Why, do you know her?
Bruce. Know her? No. You might as well ask me if I knew Proserpina.
Joel. So, if we have good success in trapping this miss—we will spare this Desmer his life—I will give you five hundred dollars down and one thousand when the job is completed. What say you to the terms?
Bruce. The terms are right enough; but the idea of risking one's life on t..e deck of a burning steamboat is not so pleasant to reflect on.
Joel. [*Aside.*] No—not so long as I foot up your bills, and give you an odd thousand. [*Aloud.*] What do we care for the lives of others as long as we run no risk? My plans are to fire the boat in a lonesome part of the river, and with the assistance of another, we can with ease abduct her. Here is five hundred to bind the bargain. [*Gives money.*]
Bruce. I agree—but how am I to get the back thousand, if you go down with the boat?
Joel. I will take good care that this don't occur. The boat that they are going on is the Reindeer, and she is advertised to leave at five. Look you to the securing of berths, I will manage the rest. Meet me at the hotel at three, and be alive to the importance of the hour. Remember I am to be disguised—and my name is Howard. [*Exit* L.]
Bruce. All right, Mr. Howard. [*Looking after him.*] There goes a man—no—not a man, but a fiend. Hell ceases to be wicked when compared to his heart. For three years have I been his constant companion— I laugh, I chat, I resort with him, and yet I could drain his heart's blood drop by drop to fill the depth of my vengeance. But the time has not yet come— one more link to complete the chain of my evidence.

Five years ago, I had a mother and a sister, the later was then scarce eighteen and as beautiful as the eyes of mortals ever looked upon, my father was a sea-captain, and on his last voyage to China, he died there. On learning of his death, I went there—but, that was a fatal hour, for, on my return, one year after, it was to find my mother on her dying-bed heart-broken. It was then and there I heard of my sister's fate: decoyed—ruined—and murdered by him. I swore by her dying-bed I would avenge my sister's death—and—I will. [*Going, meets Paris Desmer.*]

Enter PARIS DESMER, R., *looking sad.*

Why, what's the matter, my friend? you look sick.

Paris. Sick—yes I am—of a heartless and indifferent world that has no eyes to mercy, no ears to entreaty—when men's hearts are bought and sold by the paltry dollar that passes as current change.

Bruce. Are you a stranger here?

Paris. Yes sir. I came here some weeks ago on my way west. I had means to take me to my destination; but, I became a victim of some petty thief, who made his heart rejoice over my last dollar. I then sought employment—I walked these streets day and night, in search of some, but none could I get. Their plea was, you are a stranger, we don't know you. In the same city that numbers its churches by the score, and where charity is preached from every pulpit, you could starve on the marble-steps of these God-like temples, before any one would offer you aid.

Bruce. [*Much moved.*] Yes, I believe you; but don't get discouraged, all will come right. You are young and robust, keep an honest heart within your breast, and you will soon become, no matter what locality you settle in, a rich and respected man. Life is all before you, look to the future, regardless of the past.

Paris. Thank you, sir, for your counsel, I hope to profit by it. [*Going.*]

Bruce. Hold, friend, I will give you a letter to one who may be able to give you employment. [*Puts money into an envelope—writes a short note.*] Lose no time in presenting it. I wish you success.

Paris. How am I to repay this kindness?

Bruce. By being true to yourself.

Paris. This act alone would induce me to be.

[*Exit* R.]

Bruce. Thank heaven that I am able to relieve his misfortunes. When last I saw him he was but a boy. His face still wears that nobleness of soul it did then. [*Looking off* R.] Ah, here, he returns, I must be off. The letter had no address, I intended it for him.

[*Exit* L.]

Re-enter PARIS DESMER, *in haste.*

Paris. This letter is addressed to no one. Ah, he is gone. What means this—a trick, may be. No, he could not certainly have intended to deceive me, his solemn tone and good advice did not indicate it. It contains something, I will open it. May be the address is on the inside. [*Opens letter; takes out money and note.*] What! money—bank notes—there must must be some mistake here, certainly. Ah, here is a note, it may explain all. [*Reads.*] "Enclosed find two hundred dollars—it is for your use—and should we meet hereafter, recognize me not, much depends on your discretion. A friend." This I do not understand—some mystery, I know, not far off—"recognize me not if we meet again"—who can he be? I have a faint recollection of seeing him before—but where, I know not. I will be governed by his counsel—his friendship he has proved. The world is not so blank, after all, as I thought it to be. In my misery I forget thee not, my mother—nor thee, Pedestin—thy last words ere unceasingly echoed in my ears, every breeze seems the bearer. It was a terrible struggle, between duty and love, to part from you. Another such, my heart could not withstand, death itself would be a relief. But better now as it is in time, you will be content and happy. That thought alone will be a source of joy to me. [*Exit* R.]

SCENE V.—*The Cabin of the Steamboat Reindeer, well down stage so as to allow setting of Scene VI in rear. Passengers seen moving about. Storm gathering; lightning, thunder, &c.*

Enter PEDESTIN *and* ROSE.

Rose. Dear cousin, you must not feel sad. We are not so long from home yet that you should become discouraged. I feel confident that we will soon get some tidings of him.
Ped. It is not that alone, Rose, I have other fears, and yet I cannot place them. Did you notice that man with black whiskers who has been watching us so closely since we came on the boat?
Rose. No, not particularly.
Ped. [*Aside.*] When ever I look at him an inward fear takes possession of me.

Enter JOEL MERTLOFF *and* RUSSELL, L.

Joel. [*To Russell, pointing to Pedestin and Rose.*] The one this way—the fairest—mark her well.
Russell. I could not forget if I would try. She is beautiful.
Joel. Let us go, they are noticing us. [*Exit* C. D.]

Enter CUTE L.

Cute. Missie Patavine, we's gwin so fast dat de

fyer is comin' out ob de chimney ob de boat, and de trees look no bigger dan cane.

Rose. We have a fast beat—the Reindeer.

Cute. Yes, I spec so, and 'tis de fastest boat dat meets with combustin'.

Ped. Cute should any accident occur you come to your stateroom.

Cute. I will, Missie Patavine, I isn't gwin to sleep much needer. [*Thunder heard.*]

Rose. This is going to be a stormy night, cousin. We had better retire, I feel weary.

Ped. [*Aside.*] Yes, to bed, but no sleep for me.

[*Exit,* C. D.]

Cute. I'se got to keep my eyes pealed on des hyar boat, for de white folks can steal jes as well as de nigger, if nuffin better.

Enter GREEN, C. D.

Green. My colored friend, I suppose you hail from South, do you not?

Cute. Yes sah, I is.

Green. Do you ever pray down there?

Cute. Once in 'while, but when dar is cotton picking, we dusn't say none den.

Green. What kind of a field would it be for a missionary?

Cute. Missary? I dont knows what dat is, 'less 'tis stealin' niggers, and 'tis bad for dat, kase dey hang all such fellows dar.

Green. No, no, I am a minister of the gospel.

Cute. Dar's none ob dat down dar, eeder; I tinks dat you better try sum oder place.

Green. You don't understand me—I mean, a preacher of the Lord and Saviour.

Cute. O, yes, you is one of dem fellow.

Green. Yes, I teach the colored folks the way to heaven. I will now teach you the ten commandments that our Lord gave Moses on Mount Sinaii. [*Cute appears interested.*] The first com andment is, thou shalt not kill.

Cute. Yes, dat's it.

Green. Second, thou shalt keep the Sabbath-day holy.

Cute. Yes.

Green. The third, thou shalt not covet thy neighbor's goods. [*Steals Cute's pocket-book.*]

Cute. Yes.

Green. The fourth is, thou shalt not steal.

Cute. Yes, dat's so.

Green. O, I forgot there's a friend waiting for me, I'll teach you the rest to-morrow. [*Exit* R.]

Cute. Dat fellow changed his mind in a hurry. I speck he is— [*Feels for his pocket-book.*] he is—Oh, Lor' he—he stole my pocket-book. [*Runs around stage.*] No, [*Laughs.*] he didn't, I'se fooled him, I'se got de money in my shu'; dar ain't a red cent in dat book. O, golly, he didn't make much dat time. He show de nigger de way to heabben, he'll do well if he gets dar hissef. O, golly, how he am fooled! [*Exit* L.]

Enter JOEL MERTLOFF *and* BRUCE, R.

Bruce. A bad night, I fear, Joel.

Joel. Yes, but one well calculated to answer our purpose, every thing is in readiness. Three hours more and we will be on the rapids—the cry of fire there will cause such a consternation, that we can easily effect our plan without any fear of detection—the darkness of the hour will aid us, too. [*Thunder and lightning become louder and more vivid.*] This night reminds me of a similar one, which I have seen on this mighty river, near five years ago.

Bruce. [*Much interested.*] I remember of your telling me something about it, you had a girl along, I believe—

Joel. Yes, and her equal in beauty, I have not seen since.
Bruce. Beauty?—It seems that every one you speak of is a beauty.
Joel. She was queen of all.
Bruce. Did she get drowned, Joel? [*Suppressing his voice.*]
Joel. No. Everybody supposed she did.
Bruce. How, then?
Joel. You see, I got the girl dead in love with me, and after a while, I got tired of her; so, one stormy night like this, I took her in a skiff on the river with the intention of putting her under the water; but the skiff was so light that I could not do so without endangering my life, so I took her back to the shore, and—an old well answered my purpose better, for, to this day, no one knows she is lying at the bottom of it.
Bruce. Oh—my God—my—
    [*A loud clap of thunder is heard.*]
Joel. Why—what has startled you?
Bruce. Did you not feel that clap of thunder; it took my breath away—continue.
Joel. That is all. Only, at times, I fancy I see her weeping over the well.
Bruce. Is she the one you call Meralla?
Joel. No, her name was Isabel Benson.
Bruce. [*Trying to suppress himself.*] Isabel Ben—
Joel. Did you know her?
Bruce. Know her?—no. It was the oddness of the name that struck me. [*The storm increasing in fury, rain falling.*] Let's us go back, I feel a weakness coming over me from the effects of that shock. [*Going and aside.*] My evidence is now complete. A just vengeance soon will be mine.   [*Exit* C D.]

Scene VI.—*The Rapids. A steamboat seen crossing stage from* L *to the head of them; as she gets near them, is struck by lightning. Rapids cross stage right to left and recross again. The boat burns to end of scene. Cute comes down the rapids with Pedestin; after going through them, re-enters in two.*

Enter Cute, R., *carrying* Pedestin.

Cute. Oh, tank de blessed Lor', I has saved you, Missie Patavine. I has saved you, and you is not dead. [*Raises her head and kneels by her.*]

END OF ACT II.

ACT III.

Scene I.—*A set Inn (Sign Half-way.) A sign on* R, "*Ten miles to the Falls.*"

Enter Walter Bruce, L.

Bruce. [*Looks around.*] "Half-Way-House," "Ten miles to the Falls." This house is half way between the Falls and where—well, it makes no difference— I'm not going any farther for the present. The thought of that horrifying night still sickens my soul. It is seldom the "father of waters" is witness to such a sight. A boat struck by lightning loaded with human freight. Thank God, I was there, for I saved that night, the life of one whose memory is ever dear to me. Her whom I had not seen for four long years—the hope and joy of other days. I know not how I rescued her from the burning wreck, for, when I came to myself, I was on the shore and Rose Merview was saved. Cute, the faithful negro, saved Pedestin, but it was only escaping death to become a captive to Joel Mertloff, for hardly had she recovered from the shock, ere Mertloff and his accomplice abducted her, leaving the poor negro for dead, for he fought them until overpowered. Joel Mertloff, you will not taunt your victim long, for a swift and terrible retribution will soon overtake you. The just vengeance of a murdered sister will be mine.

[*Exit into Inn.*]

Enter LANDLORD *and* PARIS DESMER, L, *dressed as a hunter, with rifle, &c.*

Landlord. Let me tell you, stranger, that you never came into a better country for fishing, hunting and trapping than hereabouts. The woods are alive with game, and as you look to be a pretty clever fellow I wouldn't mind if you would become a neighbor of mine. Is your family large? I dare say a wife and two or three children.

Paris. No, sir, I have no family, I'm not married.

Landlord. So much the better. There is three or four marriagable girls in the neighborhood. Old Bob Johnson has one and 'Squire Green has another. They are well-to-do farmers, and I have two. Now, certainly out of four blooming girls you can't help getting a wife. I would like to ask you, if you have no objection, what part of the country you are from.

Paris. No, sir, I am from the South.

Landlord. Well, you are just as welcome as though you were from my native State, New Hampshire, so make yourself at home, and, after dinner, we will take a ride out, and I will show you the country, and should we have time we will drive to the falls.

Paris. Thank you, sir.

Landlord. But come, let us go in, it's 'round towards noon.

Paris. I wish to stay out a few moments longer. I desire to try my hand at targeting. I will join you presently.

Landlord. As you wish, but be on hand for dinner. [*Enter Inn.*]

Paris. That kind-hearted landlord seems to take a great interest in my welfare. He would have me married and settled before I well knew the name of the place. I will stay here for a time, and should the hunting field prove a success, I will remain all winter. I have not since seen my unknown friend and benefactor, but hope, even yet to return his kindness ten-fold. [*Going—sees Bruce is about to speak to him.*]

Enter WALTER BRUCE, *from Inn.*

Bruce. Ah, my friend, I will do the recognizing. [*Shakes his hand.*] I am glad to meet you. But, first, how came you here—any important business that called your attention?

Paris. No, not any, come here by mere chance. After parting with you I bought a hunting out-fit, and learning that this was a good country for game I left on the day following. Yesterday I arrived here.

Bruce. [*Aside.*] Then he is ignorant of all. I must inform him, for I want his aid.

Paris. Your letter and its contents I would wish—

Brure. Not a word as to it, and you will favor me. Now, as to your coming here. I think it was more for good luck than otherwise. Now, listen to me, Paris Desmer.

Paris. [*Startled.*] You know me, then?

Bruce. Yes, I do. But should you know me keep it to yourself. In time you will know all. I will now tell you news of a startling character. I hope you will bear it with prudence and fortitude, for in time you will know all.

Paris. Is it so momentous as all that?

Bruce. You will soon be a judge. But, listen. Since you left home a great change has taken place. Colonel Nortville died in London, two months ago.

Paris. Colonel Nortville dead?

Bruce. Yes. His will leaves his daughter, Pedestine, but a mere livelihood, in case she does not consent to marry one Joel Mertloff, which she determinately declines doing.

Paris. Is it possible that he disinherited his own daughter for refusing to marry this Mertloff?

Bruce. Such is the case. Subsequently, Pedestin came North, accompanied by her cousin, Rose Merview, and a servant named Cute. I am told that the object of her tour is to learn of your whereabouts.

Paris. [*Starts.*] Me. No, no. Not me.

Bruce. Yes, you. No one else.

Paris. Where are they, now?

Bruce. Not far from here.

Paris. How came she to know that I was here, and my sojourn so short?

Bruce. Love is an unerring pilot, Desmer.

Paris. [*Aside.*] She loves me still.

Bruce. The boat they came on met with an accident.

Paris. [*Starts.*] Oh, God. She is not—

Bruce. No, no. Cute saved her.

Paris. Oh! Thank heavens for that. But her cousin—

Bruce. She is safe, and cared for by a good woman not far from here. Pedestin is not quite so near, and—

Paris. And where, tell me.

Bruce. [*Aside.*] I would spare his feelings were it possible. [*Aloud.*] Oh! She was rescued from the boat by Cute, and afterward abducted by two men. Joel Mertloff was one of them.

Paris. Oh, man, you will drive me mad. She to suffer all this for me—she a captive to a demon. Oh! heaven, this is more than I have strength to bear. [*Is supported by Bruce.*]

Bruce. Cheer up. It is not half as bad as you think. Be advised by me, and you will soon have her for yourself.

Paris. For her sake, I am ready to face death. Show me but the way!

Bruce. No, not so hasty. In a day or two, Cute will be recovered, for we will need his assistance.

Paris. Cute wounded?

Bruce. Yes. He fought bravely in her defense, but they finally overpowered him and left him for dead. Be of good cheer; by to-morrow, I will have effected a plan for her release. Remain here, that I may know where to find you—and be your own counsel. [*Exit* L.]

Paris. [*Looking after him.*] Startling? Thou mightst well call thy news startling. She in the power of him who knows not mercy—the thought is terrible.

Enter CUTE, R., *walking lame, one arm tied up in a white cloth. When he sees Paris, he increases his speed.*

Cute. O, Massa Paris, [*Takes his hand.*] I'se so glad, I'se so glad to see you. Missie Patavine is carried away, and I can't lib widout her, I has fought hard to keep her, but dey took her from me. We must get her back, I'se ready to die for her. [*Much moved.*]

Paris. [*Aside.*] Poor fellow! What a faithful one he is! [*Aloud.*] Yes, Cute. To-morrow night, we will rescue her. Did they wound you badly?

Cute. No, Massa Paris. I'se near well now, 'twas

dat Joel Mertloff dat shot me, and took Missie Patavine wid anoder man. We has one friend here, I knows him long time ago, he saved Missie Rose. Don't ask me his name, kase I don't keer 'bout tellin' it. He know where Missie Patavine is, and will help us get her.

Paris. No, I won't ask you—he is our friend then.

Cute. Yes, I knows it.

Paris. Cute, remain with me, I will see that your wants are supplied.

Cute. Tankee, Massa Paris, I wills.

Paris. And by the setting of two more suns, we will, with the assistance of a just Providence, free her from her thralldom, which is worse than death.

[*Exit Inn.*]

Scene II.—*Interior of a Log House denoting strength.*

Enter Joel Mertloff *and* Granny Swabs, *door in* c.

Joel. Well, Granny, how fares my pet?

Granny. Inclined to be sulky, Mr. Mertloff. Just like all her kind. She will cool down, I think, before long—close quarters and no show of escape, is a cure in itself, to say nothing of your sweet words, and them, I know you have.

Joel. [*Trying to laugh.*] So you think I have a flattering tongue, do you, Granny? [*Gives her money.*]

Granny. 'Tis you that have: that is all you fine gentlemen study—especially handsome ones like you—when it suits your purposes.

Joel. I believe I owe you a little back change. [*Gives her more money.*]

Granny. Thank you, Mr. Mertloff, your generous heart is in keeping with your good looks—which cannot be said of every fine gentleman. You said something about letting this miss out to take a little fresh air occasionally, how about that?

Joel. We will wait a few days—too much humoring would have a bad effect. I want her to understand that she is in my power, and no hopes of getting out of it, until she accedes to my wishes, for, she will then become sensible of her position and will early realize the importance of coming to terms.

Granny. You have had a great deal of experience in such matters, your knowledge extends a long way, Mr. Mertloff.

Joel. Well—yes—I have had a little experience in my time.

Granny. I know that.

Joel. Granny, you must be careful, and not hold any long chat with her. You know that when you women's tongues get agoing, you don't know when they will stop. She is very shrewd, and might be prying you for secrets that I don't wish her to know. I now warn you of ever mentioning the name of Isabel Benson to her.

Granny. I am crafty enough for that. I have had dealing with too many of her sort to be gumed by her now.

Joel. Yes, but none as sharp as she is.

Granny. I ain't dull, neither.

Joel. I know that. I only thought to put you on your guard—good counsel is ever acceptable to the wise.

Granny. I don't object, Mr. Mertloff, no indeed.

Joel. What do you think of her—do you think a man could be happy with her—after she moderates?

Granny. Men are so changeable, that is very hard to tell.

Joel. You are becoming sarcastic, Granny. That was intended for me—I know your joking turns.

Granny. No, not for you, in particular. All men are mostly alike on that point.

Joel. It is her wealth that I am after. I don't care a fig for her beauty. [*Going.*] Tell Miss Nort-

ville that I wish to see her this morning. [*Aside.*] Bruce's absence I cannot account for. He is now away a day. Something must be amiss with him.
[*Exit door.*]

Granny. I will bear the glad tidings to her, as she terms them. As long as I fill my purse it matters not to me which way the wind blows. [*Counting the money.*] He was inclined to be generous to-day. A little blarney never hurts men. They are naturally conceited, and their vanity is easily imposed on. The longer she stays here, the better it is for me, and the prospects are now that it will be for some time. She has a mind of her own, and a strong one at that.
[*Exit* L.]

Enter MERTLOFF, *with* BRUCE, C. D.

Joel. I could not tell for the life of me what had become of you.

Bruce. When I lost my horse I had to foot it, and one makes slow headway among thickets and brush. The worst I have to tell is that I did not accomplish my mission.

Joel. You will have to make another trip, then.

Bruce. Yes, and to-night, which makes me sick of this country life. [*Gruffly.*]

Joel. Don't be discouraged, young man, nothing was ever accomplished in a day. You are indulging in another fit of the blues—that no sensible minded person is ever troubled with. You must have been born in twilight, when the spirit of uneasiness is said to rule supreme.

Bruce. [*Aside.*] Nor will I until I see you swing from the gallows. [*Aloud.*] I happened to be of a city turn of mind, Joel, backwood life and me don't agree, but then I think that I can stand it as long as you can. That is, if she don't wear us both out. What think you?

Joel. Not she, I think I notice a change in her already.

Bruce. Good. The sooner the better.

Joel. You have heard nothing as to the fate of her cousin. You remember of seeing her when the boat was in flames?

Bruce. No, I do not. The falling of that timber on me cut my recollection short, for when I recovered my senses I lay on the shore, shivering from the night air.

Joel. That negro, Cute, have you heard anything of him?

Bruce. No. I suppose that he is dead.

Joel. I hope so. He fought like a tiger. I had to shoot him twice. [*Pedestin and Granny heard outside.*] Ah, here come her ladyship.

Bruce. Then I will leave. [*Aside.*] Now, to give her this letter [*shows letter*] unseen by him. [*As he is going out, she enters; he hands her the letter.*]

Enter PEDESTIN, C. D.

Joel. Ah, Miss Pedestin, I thank you for your alacrity. I did not look for you so soon. May I hope that you are in more settled state of mind this morning? Your appearance goes far to indicate it.

Ped. Mock me, with your scoffing tongue, if it be your pleasure. Flattery and reproach are seasoned alike by your lips. I am no longer the weak, ineffectual one you thought me. I fear you not, Mertloff. Do your worst—a man, whose soul is so debased by sin as yours, is a poltroon to his actions.

Joel. [*Aside.*] Ha, ha, showing you true colors, are you? so will I hoist mine. [*Aloud.*] I am not desirous of entering into a controversy, this morning. Tongue-slashing is not my forte. I wished to spare your feelings all I possibly could; but as you seem open to discord, my clemency is rendered unavailable.

Now to be plain with you. Pedestin, you are hopelessly in my power—not the remotest show of deliverance. I have solemnly sworn that you will be my wife. To keep that oath, I have abducted you here, fully resolved on your retention, until you consent to become mine. I would counsel you to prudence, and beg you to submit to reason. Ere many days have passed, you will see the wisdom of an early compliance.

Ped. When the midnight assassin casts aside his mask, his true character is known—so it is with you, Joel Mertloff, I see you now unveiled. You give me to understand that I am in your power—your captive—and I am to remain here until I gratuitously consent to marry you. O, man, fiend—or whatever you are—do you think, by confining me here, you will induce me to become your wife? No—go set my prison-walls in flames, for, sooner would I be buried among their smouldering ruins, than live and bear the stigma of your name. [*Change sides.*]

Joel. I am sorry to see you thus dictated by a so irresistible mind, for, no good will come from it. The longer you strive to evade the issue, the more rebellious will this spirit become. You know that it was your father's wish that we should be married, and to make it more infallible, at his dying hour, he stipulated it in his will.

Ped. I wish, sir, you would spare my father's name—his memory should at least be held sacred—and, though he did acquiesce in my marriage, I am compelled to treat it as naught.

Joel. Oh, well, if you are as persistent as all that, you will be the sufferer.

Ped. I may be for a time, Mertloff, but mark me, a swift and terrible retribution will soon overtake you. Pride yourself on my forcible retention here—brave—noble—generous man that you are. It is an insult to man's form, that you have his shape—you who believe not in sacrificing Love on Hymen's altar.

Joel. If thus be your bent, I will leave you. My argument is shivered to atoms by your womanly tongue; but, remember, Pedestin Nortville, that out of this house, you never shall go, until you consent to be mine, or unless it be to your grave.

[*Exit door.*]

Ped. To my grave be it, then!

Enter GRANNY SWABS.

Granny. Come, miss to your room, I can't leave you alone here—Mr. Mertloff's orders are strict, and must be complied with.

Ped. I suppose his orders are rigid; but, granny, you will leave me here a few moments, it is so much more pleasant here than in that dark room.

Granny. I would, if I could; but, you see, I cant. I will do all I can for your comfort.

Ped. Thank you, granny, I am sure you will. Has Mr. Mertloff had this place long?

Granny. For some time, I believe.

Ped. Had he ever any one confined here as I am?

Granny. This is a question I don't care about answering.

Ped. [*Gives her money.*] You know we must talk about something.

Granny. Well, as it is you—and I know you won't say anything about it—I will tell you.

Ped. I won't say a word.

Granny. He had three here.

Ped. [*Starts.*] Three, here!

Granny. Yes, but none for two years till you came.

Ped. What became of them?

Granny. That, I can't really say. He took them

away, and that was the last I ever saw or heard of them.
Ped. Do you remember their names?
Granny. No. You see, they didn't stay here long, and 'tis over two or three years ago, I forget which, since the last one was here. They were not as pretty as you are, but they were mild and gentle girls.
Ped. Why, granny—ain't I mild and gentle?
Granny. Mr. Mertloff says not. I suppose he must know—he has more dealing with you than I have. But, then, I like you for that—I like to see a woman stand up for her right and speak her mind right out, as you do—these crying girls, I have no use for. I think Mr. Mertloff found his match in you.
Ped. What makes you think so, granny?
Granny. I heard you talking to him—none of the other girls ever was that bold—he did the talking, and they the crying. But I see there is none of that around you.
Ped. No, granny, I don't shed my tears here. [*Aside.*] Oh, I forgot about the letter I got from that strange man, as I came in. [*Aloud.*] Granny, [*Gives money.*] will you get me a drink of water?—I am so thirsty.
Granny. Certainly. I will—and any favor I can do for you, just let me know it. [*Aside.*] I am getting to like that girl better and better every day—and she has plenty of money, too, which makes her still worthier of kindness. [*Counting money.*] and she knows how to use it—which a heap of folks don't.
[*Exit door.*]
Ped. Now for the contents of that letter. [*Opens letter and reads:*] "Your deliverance from captivity will be before the setting of another sun. Hold yourself in readiness—make no ostentation, so that suspicion may not arise—for much depends on your part. Your friends are not far distant,

and, he who gave you this, will lead them to your rescue.   YOUR UNKNOWN FRIEND.

"P. S.—I would say more, did I not fear that joy would override your prudence."

[*Thoughtfully.*] He "would say more, did he not fear that joy would override prudence," Can I believe—can I hope? No, no—I dare not encourage the thought—it would be hoping too much, 'Tis well that he did not, for, were it so, I could not contain myself. My cousin, then, was saved, and poor Cute, to whom I owe my life, is not dead. [*Wipes her eyes.*] I must not show any sign of tears when granny comes in, she might suspect something wrong. Now, to be as cool and indifferent as a man hanging, I mean, after he is hung. If I could but know the time of day—

Re-enter GRANNY SWABS, *with a glass of water.*

Oh, granny, [*Unthinkingly.*] what time is— [*Granny starts, spills water.*] I mean, what kind of water have you?

Granny. "What kind of water have I?" 'Tis on the floor now, and you can judge for yourself.

Ped. Oh, granny, I did not mean to startle you; however, I will do without it now, I do not wish to tax your kindness.

Granny. Oh, no, you won't—I would not deny any creature a drink.

Ped. Never mind, granny. I will go with you to my room, I feel a faintness coming on me from the excitement of this morning.

Granny. As you wish, my dear; but I hope you will not get sick. You will have one comfort—if you should—

Ped. What?—

Granny. There will be no danger of your dying.

Ped. How do you make that out, granny?

Granny. Why, we have no doctors about these diggings.

Ped. [*Aside.*] Freedom will cure me. My heart will count each fleeting moment, as they take their leave and my lips kiss them good-bye.

[*Exit both, door.*]

Scene III.—*Same as Scene I, Act III.*

Enter Landlord, *from Inn.*

Landlord. Well, I don't see what in the world has got into that young man, Mr.—Mr.—what is this he calls himself?—Well it don't matter, He is as uneasy as a crab out of water. He has been here three days and has not sat down, laid down, or eaten anything as yet, which is well for my pocket. And, what is more strange, he is continually in the company of my daughters; just as I was when I was sparking. Swivel me if I don't think he is in love with Betty. I know that she is struck right down in love with him. Well, 'tis no wonder, he's a handsome feller. If they should get married I will set them right down on that small farm across the creek, and let them hoe out a future for themselves, as I did with less help. Then, if I find him a right good son-in-law, I will let him and Betty run the "Half-Way," when they carry me to the bone-yard, although I don't think that will be for a dozen years yet.

Enter Walter Bruce, L.

Bruce. Ah, landlord, good day.
Landlord. The same to you, sir.
Bruce. Landlord, can't you tell me where I would be most apt to get the loan of a skiff that would carry about four persons? I want to use it only one night.

Landlord. That is pretty hard to get around here. I have one, but I don't care about letting it out. I had one broken on me, and to this day I never got a red for it.

Bruce. [*Gives him money.*] Well, you see I am an old sailor and always keep a weather-eye to breakers ahead.

Landlord. If that's the case, I don't mind if you do take the boat for the night, but take good care of it and be sure that you don't forget to return it.

Bruce. I will reef her should a gale come up, and if the storm continue, I will cast anchor on dry land.

Landlord. All right. I see you understand the ropes. You will find the boat ready when you are.

[*Exit door.*]

Bruce. So much accomplished. Now to see Desmer and Cute, and then for the finale. Mertloff, I believe, is half way on the alert. Whether he surmises anything amiss or not, he keeps it to himself. I was lucky in getting so favorable an opportunity to give Pedestin Nortville the letter. I told her nothing of young Desmer, fearful that, in the joy of the moment, she would be thrown off her guard.

Enter DESMER *and* CUTE. *Both are about to speak.*
BRUCE, *seeing them, comes forward.*

Bruce. My friends, leave that to me. I am glad to see you both.

Paris. And we are no less to see you, sir.

Cute. We is dat, massa, [*brings hand to mouth*] for Massa Paris is all de time frettin' 'bout Missie Patavine. We is ready to get her.

Bruce. That will be to-night.

Paris. To-night? Thank you, friend, that is welcome news. Show us but the way, you will find our valliancy worthy of the prize.

Bruce. I doubt it not. I have all in readiness—I

have a boat at our command—Pedestin, too, is forewarned of the rescue, and will act accordingly. See that you are well armed, for, should you meet resistance, you will have to use them.

Paris. I will look to that.

Cute. I'se all right. [*Shows pistol.*] I has got dis hyar to cook his goose, if he show his mug dar.

Bruce. The place of her confinement is not so very far but is difficult of access. It is situated among thicket and brush; there is but one path leading there, and that is on the verge of a deep ravine. I have a trusty horse for Pedestin's use, give him free rein, and I warrant that he will guide you safe to the river.

Paris. So near, and yet in his power.

Bruce. Not after to-night. Should I make a faint show of resistance, after you are beyond pursuit, remember I do it to ward off suspicion—I have not yet settled accounts with him. There is no time now to be lost. Meet me at the boat in one hour—we must cross the river and gain the path before it is dark.

Paris. [*Aside.*] An hour—oh—my heart already seems pennoned by a thousand wings that would fain bear it on afore.

Bruce. Remember the time, now or never.

[*Exit* R.]

Paris. Now be it, then. [*Exit* L.]

Cute. [*Showing pistol.*] I will load her to de muzzle, and I'll gib his goose cookin', dat will last him.

[*Exit* R.]

Enter LANDLORD, *in haste.*

Landlord. Well, if that young man, my intended son-in-law hasn't put everything and everybody in a complete tumult. He is running from post to pillar —loading and reloading pistols—I suppose that he meditates suicide, or somebody's side, from the way he is carrying on. And to make it worse, he has got my daughter Betty in equally as uneasy a state of mind—for, she is kind of sweet on the fellow—[*Bugle heard.*] Ah, there is the seven o'clock stage—that means business. [*Exit Inn.*]

Scene IV.—*A steep precipice—high rocks on both sides. There must be a bridge or plank across from side to side, that will bear the weight of two, and can easily knocked away, after Desmer, Pedestin and Cute have crossed it. Cataract in the distance. Further up, the precipice becomes winding, and path leading up to the* L.

Enter Joel Mertloff *and* Russell, *mouth of precipice,* L.

Joel. There is my secret pass, Russell. [*Pointing to bridge.*] I have often baffled pursuit by crossing there—it saves five miles of a round—which is a great deal in a country like this.

Russell. Yes, it is that.

Joel. It is already passed midnight, I know that Bruce has returned and is waiting for us. [*Going.*] Mind your steps here, see that your footing is secure, you would not feel the better of a fall.

[*Exit both by winding path.*]

Enter Bruce, Paris *and* Cute, *mouth of precipice,* L.

Bruce. This pass will take us to the rear of the house where Pedestin is confined. I hope we will get her off before Mertloff is aware of your presence. See that pathway: [*Pointing to bridge across ravine.*] I would have Cute guard it, for, should you be pursued, cross there, and then knock the structure

away—it is but a temporary one, and you will have several miles the advantage over your pursuers.
Paris. That will be as you wish.
Cute. [*Pulling out pistol.*] I'll guard dat, massa. Nebber fear—and I'll help Massa Paris, too.
Bruce. This way. [*Going.*]
Paris. [*Aside.*] To the haven of my love!
Bruce. See that you do not miss a step—to fall here would cost a life. [*They descend by winding path—Cute at the path-way on top.*] This is your post, Cute, see that you guard it. Speak low for there is the house. Paris will be back presently. [*Disappears.*]
Cute. I guards it to de last. Now to [*holds out pistol*] cook his goose—— [*Looking off L.*] Dis way, dis way, Massa Paris. He's got her—he's coming. Dis way—oh—dey am after him. [*Rushes off to meet him.*]

[*Re-appear* CUTE, PARIS *carrying Pedestin.*

Cute. Cross hyar, Massa Paris, cross hyar. [*Mertloff, Russell and Bruce heard behind. Paris crosses carrying Pedestin, Cute follows. Just as they are across, appear Mertloff, Russell and Bruce. Mertloff is about to step on the bridge-way, when Cute knocks it away. Cute defies them in dumb show.*]
Paris. Thank heaven, she is saved!

END OF ACT III.

ACT IV.

Scene I.—*A Plain Room.*

Enter Cute, l.

Cute. We is all to home 'gain, and Massa Paris, too, and I'se so glad ob it. Dar no place like home, arter all—trabeling I'se got no use for, on de boat, 'pecially, dey is all smoke and water. Missie Patavine is so glad now, dat she am laffin' all de time. I 'spec dat her and Massa Paris is soon—

Enter Pedestin, *unseen by* Cute, l.

gwine to get married, kase dey both lub each odder, dat I knows. Won't I hab a good time, den?

Ped. Won't you, though? [*Laughing.*]

Cute. [*Starts.*] Ah, Missie Patavine, I'se jus tinkin' dat—

Ped. You would have a good time at our wedding, eh?

Cute. Yes, dat's it.

Ped. I hope you will, indeed.

Cute. So does I.

Ped. Cute, I wish you to go to the village. Here are two letters—one for Mr. Mason, and the other for— [*Gives letters.*]

Cute. I knows—don't tell me. I takes dem right 'way, dis one for Massa Mason, and dat one for Massa Paris. I'll put one in dis pocket and de oder in dat, so I'se shu' to hab dem right.

Ped. Yes, that's right, make no mistake in them.

Cute. I'll know dem 'part. One is 'bout business, and de oder 'bout lub. [*Exit singing*, l.]

Ped. [*Looding after him.*] I owe him a debt of gratitude that I am powerless to pay.

Enter ROSE, R. C.

Rose. Well, cousin, is not home after all, truly delightful? Do you remember the beautiful words, "There is no place like home"? [*Sings "Sweet Home."*]

Ped. No—not after a journey like ours, Rose.

Rose. True. And what an ordeal one it was. Were not all forcibly impressed on my mind, I would fain think of it as some delusive dream; but—how happily it resulted! I know that you feel happy now, and, in that thought, I, too, find [*Sighs.*] some comfort.

Ped. Thank you, cousin. But how is it that you seem so changed since our return? You seem to be all absorbed in mind.

Rose. And so I am. I cannot drive the thought from my mind, that our rescuer was no less a personage than Walter Benson, once my plighted lover.

Ped. Is it possible?

Rose. Yes. I cannot be mistaken—for, I felt his lips touch mine, ere he thought I had recovered—and—I heard him utter my name.

Ped. Then, it must have been him. But, why didn't he make himself known to you?

Rose. This is the mystery. He was in disguise—I could see that by his misplaced wig—for, he wore one.

Ped. In disguise? That obscures the mystery more. What could be his motive for that?

Rose. That is the subject of my thoughts; but I fail to discern anything.

Ped. Do you think he still loves you?

Rose. Yes, I feel confident of it. And would you believe, that I dreamed of him last night, and that he named our wedding-day?

Ped. Then, you dream will be true, as it was he, who named it.

Rose. May heaven grant that it will!

Ped. I have sent Cute with a letter to Mr. Mason. He is to settle my portion of the will, to-day. I am looking for him every moment. It is the only obstacle that would further delay—

Rose. Your marriage. Then, remove it at once. I will hail with joy the hour that will see your happiness consumated. [*Exit* L.]

SCENE II.—*A Set Cottage.*

Enter PARIS *and* BRUCE, L.

Paris. Assist you? Yes, ask me to hazard my life, and see if I'd refuse.

Bruce. No, I would not look for that. Aid me but in this, and you will have fully repaid me.

Paris. Here is my hand on it. [*Gives hand.*]

Bruce. The well we must find first. It is some where near the river bank, and has not been used for years. Do you remember of there being such a one in the neighborhood?

Paris. Yes, I do. It must be the willow well. It is neartly full of brush, and is close by the river bank.

Bruce. That must be the one where her body has mouldered. My poor sister—!

Paris. But it will not remain there longer. It will now bear witness to convict the foul assassin—

Bruce. And by to-morrow, I will have him dragged, fettered, to prison, and show the world a fiend whose equal never inhabited human shape.

Paris. [*Starts.*] Mertloff at home!

Bruce. Yes, he returned last night, but few know it.

Paris. Does he not suspect your true character?
Bruce. No—not he. It was but this morning, he proposed to me a plot to take your life—but be not uneasy as to that, I will see that you run no danger. Meet me to-night at nine, I will wait for you at the bridge.
Paris. I will be there, you may depend on it. [*Exit Bruce,* L.] He plots against my life—it is no more than I expected to hear. But, thank heaven, a well-merited retribution will soon overtake him.

Enter MRS. DESMER, *from cottage, with a letter.*

Mrs. D. Why, Paris, where have you been? Dinner is cold—waiting for you.
Paris. I intended to be back sooner, mother; but I met a friend, and he detained me.
Mrs. D. Cute has been here and left a letter for you. [*Gives letter.*] Here it is.
Paris. [*Aside.*] It is from her, I know. [*Opens it.*]
Mrs. D. Paris, I would like to speak with you— if you have leisure time.
Paris. Certainly, mother—my time is yours.
Mrs. D. But you have not read your letter.
Paris. There is nothing very urgent in it, I don't think.
Mrs. D. Paris, I have a matter of great importance to communicate to you, and I know not how to broach it. Do not censure me—for one word of reproach from you, would almost break my heart. I love you as well as if you were my own son—
Paris. [*Starts.*] I, not your son—oh! mother, you are not serious. No, no, you can not be—
Mrs. D. Yes, Paris, I am. Do not turn away from me—stay and hear me through. I know that I acted wrong; but I could not help it. Though I am not your mother, I have tried to be one to you—

Paris. I know you have, and I forgive you—your kindness has ever made you a mother to me.

Mrs. D. Bless you for that. I will tell you all, and you will blame me less. Twenty years ago, my husband and I, with an infant daughter then five months old, were on our way West. The boat we were on met with an accident, near these shores. Nearly all on board were lost. I leaped from the boat with my babe in my arms—and, when I came to my senses, I was in a hut, and my child gone. It was about a month after, that an old negro told me he had found my child on the shore—almost lifeless—and carried it to the residence of Colonel Nortville. Mrs. Nortville, at that time, had twins—a boy and a girl—the age of mine. It so happened that her infant daughter died the night that mine was brought there. So, unknown to any one—save that old negro—she adopted my child, and said that mine died instead of hers. I was determined on regaining my child, for I had no one now—my husband was drowned. One night I entered the house—and, unseen by any one, I stole to the cradle where my babe and her son were sleeping. In my confusion, I took the wrong one—it was her son—you, George Nortville—

Paris. [*Starts.*] Me—George Nortville! Oh, no, not I—

Mrs. D. Yes, you—Paris. You are sole heir to your father's wealth. Pedestin is my daughter—I have your mother's dying confession of the facts. Will you forgive me, now that you know how much I am to blame?

Paris. Forgive you? O, yes, I forgive you—and you will be my mother still. [*They embrace.*]

Mrs. D. Heaven bless you. [*Takes papers from her pocket.*] I expect Mr. Mason here every moment. These are the papers to prove your parentage. Here he comes now. [*Looking off*, L.]

Enter LAWYER MASON, L.

Mason. Good-day, Mrs. Desmer. [*To Paris.*] This is your son—I mean—Mr. George Nortville.
Mrs. D. Yes, Mr. Mason, he is.
Mason. Then, Mr. Nortville, I am happy to congratulate you on your good fortune. [*They shake hands.*]
Paris. Thank you, sir.
Mrs. D. Here are the papers I spoke of, [*gives papers*] Mr. Mason.
Mason. Now, let us proceed to business. I have yet to acquaint Miss Pedestin Nortville—I mean Desmer—of these facts, for, her right to any part of the estate becomes null and void. Mr. Nortville, we will need your presence in this matter. [*Exit both in* C.]
Paris. O, heaven, can this be true? I—George Nortville—a millionaire. [*Exit in* C.]

SCENE III.—*A Street in the Village.*

Enter MERTLOFF *and* BRUCE, L.

Joel. A thousand dollars is yours the moment the job is done. You run no risk whatever—you are not known here—therefore, you are the last one that would be suspected. You cannot make it easier. Make up you mind, and see me to-morrow at Morsay. [*Going.*]
Bruce. [*Looking off* R, *anxiously.*] Stay, I may make up my mind now. [*Aside.*] I expect the officers every moment. [*Aloud.*] You say, one thousand dollars—
Joel. Yes, one thousand. If I cannot hire it done, I will do it myself, for, I have sworn that he should not live to make her his wife.

Bruce. [*Looking off* R.] Couldn't you make it five hundred more? The job is worth it.

Joel. Well, I will give five hundred more. But, remember, you must make a clean thing of it.
[*Going.*]

Paris. Hold, I wouldn't care if you would give me a few hundred as bonus. [*Looking off* R.]

Joel. All right. Here is three hundred dollars. I hope this will satisfy you. The rest when the work is done. [*Going.*]

Bruce. Here, you made a mistake. [*Counting money.*] There's only two hundred here. [*Gives money back.*]

Joel. [*Counting money.*] Yes, there's three hundred here. [*Offers it back.*]

Bruce. [*Looking off* R. *Aside.*] Ah, here they come. [*Offers money again. Aloud.*] No, keep your sordid dollars—your own hands are better fit than mine to do such work—

Joel. What mean you?

Bruce. They will tell you. [*Pointing to officers.*]

Enter Two Officers, R.

Officer. Joel Mertloff, I arrest you, in the name of the State, on the charge of murder.

Joel. [*Starts.*] Me—charged with murder! And whom have I murdered?

Officer. Isabel Benson, whose body was found in willow well.

Joel. [*Staggers back.*] Isabel Benson. Who dares charge me with her murder?

Bruce. [*Throwing off disguise.*] I—Walter Benson—her brother.

Joel. [*Startled.*] You—Walter Benson!

Bruce. Yes, I—who swore to avenge a murdered sister. Now, mark the fulfillment of that oath. [*Points to the officers.*]

Joel. You, infamous traitor—insidious fiend—if this be your plotting—

Enter CUTE, *followed by* VILLAGERS, L.

Take this as your reward—— [*Takes pistol out of his pocket, fires at Bruce. Cute, who is standing behind him, knocks up his arm.*]
Cute. You has murdered enough to hang twice. [*The officers seize Joel and force him off* R. Villagers shouting. *Exit after him.*]
Bruce. Cute, you have saved my life. How am I to thank you?
Cute. I'se glad, Massa Bruce, dat I was dar to do it—
Bruce. I am Bruce no more from to-day. My oath is fulfilled. Sister, thou art avenged!
[*Exit both* R.]

SCENE IV.—*A furnished apartment.*

Enter PEDESTIN *and* ROSE, C.

Ped. No, Rose, I am no longer Pedestin Nortville. Mr. Mason says I forfeit all now—even the name.
Rose. And you are not my cousin, neither.
Ped. No. [*Weeps.*]
Rose. Don't cry for that, dear Pedestin, I will love you just as well as though you were. But how strange for Mrs. Desmer to be your mother, and Paris Des——, I mean, George Nortville to be the lawful heir.
Ped. [*More cheerful.*] Yes, I was forgetting that—mistaking tears of joy for sorrow. Oh; thank thee, heaven, that thou hast rendered unto him what is his—and gave me a mother.

Rose. Yes, and I think all is for the best, dear, and, if I mistake not, you will [*laughing*] ultimately be Mrs. Pedestin Nortville.

Ped. No, no, Rose—not now. His wealth makes a channel between us not to be spanned. I hold him not to his promise—he is free now to choose another.

Rose. But he will not. His sudden accession to wealth will not change him. If his love was ever true, this will be but to gloss it. [*Aside.*] Still, it is hard to trust him—he is a man and, of course, has their traits. [*Exit* c.]

Enter CUTE, L.

Cute. Missie Patavine, I jus been to de billage, and dey are trying dat Joel Mertloff for dat murder. I 'spec dat dey will hang him. Massa Paris, and his moder is comin' obber hyar, and an'der gemman, too. [*Aside.*] Massa Benson.

Ped. Coming here? [*Sadly.*]

Cute. Yes, Missie Patavine, ain't you glad?

Ped. O, yes, I am. I have no more right here, Cute; I must now seek another home, and earn my bread by labor.

Cute. No, you isn't, 'long as I'se got dese two hands, I'll work for you, and earn you bread. [*Puts out hands.*]

Ped. But I lose you, also, Cute. They leave me nothing.

Cute. [*Moved.*] No, dey can't, kase Massa Kurnel he gib me to you 'fore he went away. I knows dat dat dey can't take me, I is yours, in spite ob dem.

Ped. I will keep you, Cute, though I should have to sell my jewels to beg you back.

Cute. I'se glad ob dat, for, I hates to part wid you, Missie Patavine. I'll work for you a long time, dough I'se ole. [*Exit* R.]

Enter PARIS *and* MRS. DESMER, L.

Ped. Mrs. Des—, oh! my mother, [*Rushes into her arms.*] my dear mother.
Mrs. D. Then, you forgive me, dear daughter.
Ped. Forgive you, dear mother? You have done nothing to ask forgiveness for.
Mrs. D. Bless you, dearest child; I was afraid you might think me guilty of blame.
Ped. No, mother, no—you are not to be blamed.
Mrs. D. Oh, how I have longed for this hour—that I might fold you to my heart, and call you daughter.
Ped. Yes, mother, your love for me has often betrayed itself; but—come, let us leave here. [*To Paris.*] Mr. Nortville, I now resign all to you. Too long have you been deprived of your own—though it was unknowingly held. I wish you joy and happiness. [*Going.*]
Paris. What Pedestin? You do not mean to ignore me now?
Ped. You are free to choose another, whose station is in accordance with your own. [*Aside.*] May heaven guide you! [*Aloud. Moved.*] Come, mother. [*Going.*]
Paris. [*Goes before her.*] You will not go. No, you will not leave here. Oh, do not, for mercy's sake draw the cords tighter—my heart is not proof against this.
Ped. No, I will not, dear Paris. Forgive me. [*They embrace.*] It was cruel in me, to think that fortune would have changed you.
Paris. Yes, Pedestin, I forgive you. It is for you alone that I prize this wealth. O, hallowed be this hour!
Mrs. D. I will leave you now, my children, and I bless you both. [*Going.*]

Ped. and Paris. No, no, mother, you will share our home.

Enter Rose *and* Walter Bruce, l.

Rose. I understand all now, dear Walter, you broke off our engagement to avenge a murdered sister.
Bruce. Yes, dear Rose.
Rose. I never will forgive myself. The men are not as bad as I thought they were.

Re-enter Cute, l.

Cute. Massa Mertloff has cooked his own goose—he's done gone, and committed susencide.
All. Mertloff—dead?
Cute. Yes, he's plum blowed out his brain—
Bruce. And cheated the gallows.
Ped. Now, Cute, for your faithful services, we will give you your liberty.
Cute. No, Missie Patavine, all de 'berty I wants, is to lib wid you and Massa Paris, all de rest ob my days.
Ped. Then, Cute, you will.
Cute. Den, I'se happy.
Paris. Ditto I, while thou, Pedestin, art the same.
Ped. I, too, Paris, if the audience deems me [worthy of the name.

r.) *Cute, Bruce, Rose,* Ped, *Paris, Mrs. D.* (l.

THE END.

www.ingramcontent.com/pod-product-compliance
Lightning Source LLC
Chambersburg PA
CBHW022148090426
42742CB00010B/1425